ONE IN A B1LLION

ONE
IN A B1LLION

*Finding Your **Genius Talent***

JOHN HITTLER

LIONCREST
PUBLISHING

ONE IN A BILLION

Finding Your Genius Talent

ISBN   978-1-5445-0201-4 *Paperback*
   978-1-5445-0202-1 *Ebook*

This book is dedicated to my two fabulous partners, Paul Leboffe and Hal Yang, who helped take a rough process, improve it, and make it much more accessible for talented human beings. This book and the genius talent discovery process would not exist without their contributions.

CONTENTS

THE NO-NONSENSE, NO BS DISCLAIMER

We designed this genius talent discovery process to be done with other people for one simple reason: you can't do it by yourself! We tried (and tried and tried), and it didn't work because the process requires you to notice, identify, and examine your blind spots, and by definition, you can't see your own blind spots; you need other people to point them out so you can proceed past them.

We've had some incredibly self-aware people attempt to work through the process on their own without any real success. One person even took a ninety-day sabbatical and worked on it thirty to forty hours a week, but he only became increasingly confused. After all that work, he ended up with numerous possibilities and no way to know for sure which was most accurate—kind of like having multiple personalities. You need to have someone who's neutral say, "Let me ask you a few questions about that" or "What did you mean by ____?" Human beings are not capable of seeing past their blind spots. As my wife says, "Your only blind spot is thinking you have none."

We also suggest working through this process with people you don't know. When you team up with friends, family, and coworkers you know well, you're biased by definition. You come to the process with preconceived notions about yourself and your partners, and this familiarity can actually hinder authentic discovery. That's not to say you can't find your genius talent when working with colleagues or friends, but from experience we know the quality of your statement will not be as high.

That said, there are five options for going through the process of discovering your genius talent, with considerations regarding time, money, and quality of the genius talent statement produced:

1. Professionally Facilitated: You can hire a trained coach to take you through the process one-on-one, rather than with a group. This option costs the most, but also takes the least amount of time—one two-hour video call. If your time is valuable or you simply want more privacy, this option is by far the most efficient. You'll get the highest quality statement with the least time invested.

2. Commando Squad—Unhosted: You can be matched up with two partners and go through the process together using this book and the website. You'll definitely put in some work and you'll meet for approximately five two-hour video calls. At the same time, however, you'll meet new people and have a great time. Most people choose the commando squad option because the process is fun to take on with partners. This option is affordable (the cost of the book only) and should create a great outcome. For the reasons mentioned previously, if you try the commando squad with friends or family, your final outcome will likely not be as accurate.

3. Commando Squad—Facilitated: You can hire an embedded guide—a trained coach who can help with the second half of the process. Your commando squad could share the investment, receive guidance, and shorten the overall time the process takes. This option offers the safety net of available help in case it's needed. Having a guide also moves the process along more quickly, so you can probably finish in four ninety-minute calls. The guide can be engaged for all or part of the process. Again, you should end up with a high-quality statement using this option.

4. One-Day Seminar: You can attend a one-day seminar and go through the process through a combination of group facilitation and a commando squad. This option involves a time investment of eight hours, as

well as travel to the seminar site. Alternatively, you can have our team work onsite with your company. Either way, you'll enjoy a Genius Talent Discovery Day and end up with a great result.

5. Swimming in the Swamp with Gators: You can ignore the warnings and attempt the process by yourself. This would be as much fun as swimming with a family of hungry alligators or joining a pack of wolves with a pork chop wrapped around your neck. It's not that success is impossible, but our experience is that even if you find a great talent, you'll have no way to validate that you are correct, unless you were pretty sure of what your talent is before you started. Still, some of you will insist on going it alone. Just remember: we warned you.

This book is written for those who choose options 2 or 3. If you would rather stop right now and hire a coach, go to www.oneinabillionbook.com. You'll be guided to a code for a discount on your private, professionally facilitated genius talent discovery process. If you're still not sure, read on. You can make up your mind after investigating a bit. Worst case, you'll learn the process before you start working with a coach.

INTRODUCTION

When I was growing up, my family had two unspoken rules: (1) Graduate from college; (2) Start saving money from the womb to pay for college. My eight siblings and I all started working very young, and by the time I was eighteen, I had saved $12,000.

In 1980, I went off to a small liberal arts college and used $6,000 of my hard-earned life savings to pay for the first year. This college was my backup choice; my first choice had been Georgetown University, but I wasn't accepted. I didn't really want to go to the liberal arts college and hadn't even bothered to visit it ahead of time. When I arrived on the first day, I discovered that it was a Baptist school with some pretty strict rules, most of which were not to my liking. A few days after the semester started, I knew the school just wasn't for me. I'm more attuned to bending and breaking strict rules than abiding by them.

Plus, I was just not willing to waste half of my life savings to pay for a college I disliked.

A week later, I was sitting in a pickup truck with my dad and my new girlfriend of five days, making the two-and-a-half-hour drive from school back to our house—in absolute dead silence. My dad is pretty hard to rattle, but you could imagine his frustration with me, quitting so soon. His attitude was heard loudly and clearly in his deafening silence. No radio. No conversation. Just silence. About two blocks from our house, my dad finally said, "Have you thought about your next move?" Of course I hadn't. I was eighteen, and I had just dropped out of school on gut instinct. I had no idea what I was doing.

Two days later, my girlfriend and I boarded the Amtrak out of Detroit and disembarked in Palo Alto, California, where my girlfriend's family lived. Palo Alto seemed infinitely preferable to Detroit. Within six months, my girlfriend was pregnant and I was swinging a pickaxe twelve hours a day for $5.50 an hour. One blazing hot day in July it hit me: *This situation is going to kill me. What do I do now?*

"What do you think about driving across the country?" I asked my girlfriend. She had been accepted at the New School for Social Research in New York City. I wanted to try again to go to Georgetown University, even though I hadn't reapplied or been accepted into the freshman class. Of course, when I proposed the plan to my girlfriend, I may have left out this key detail—I would figure out that technicality later. In mid-August 1981, we bought a 1965 VW bug, packed up what little we had, and drove to New York. My pregnant girlfriend settled into a campus apartment near the school, and I continued on to Washington, DC.

On registration day, I went to the Georgetown administrative offices to see what I could do about enrolling. The place was chaotic, with students standing in lines, confused, excited, and clueless all at the same time. I knew the incoming class consisted of roughly 1,900 students. Statistically speaking, I figured at least one person in that group was not going to show up, which would leave an open spot for me. I just needed to find someone in the registrar's office who would buy in to my simple idea of filling a vacant spot. As I mentioned earlier, I like to bend the rules, especially when they seem arbitrary.

The first person I talked to said, "What the heck are you doing? Get outta here. It doesn't work that way. You're holding up the line." Note to self: don't talk to that person again.

I got in a different line and talked to a different person, who said, "Why don't you apply for next fall, or maybe even January and come back and see us in three months."

"Okay," I said. "But, could I just come back in a couple days instead?"

"Sure, come back in a few days," the person said with a sigh, assuming her blow off would solve the immediate problem of me slowing her line.

Two days later I walked back in and explained my theory to yet another person. "Surely there must be people who didn't show up," I said.

"Well, yes, but we don't really know who they are," the person replied.

As he said this, I noticed a piece of paper lying on the desk, facing away from me. Sure enough, it was a list of people who didn't show up, and it had four names in alphabetical order, it seemed. I could only read the top one. "Well, what about Baldwin?" I asked. "Could I take Baldwin's spot?"

"How the hell did you know—" The person stopped, looked down at the desk, and moved the papers around so I could no longer see anything.

Now the real game started, as far as I was concerned. The person said, "Well, Baldwin is in the School of Foreign Service. I can't just let you into the School of Foreign Service." Of Georgetown's five different schools, the School of Foreign Service was both the most prestigious and the hardest to get into. That would be off limits, it seemed. Still, there were four other colleges, so there had to be open slots in one of those.

"What if I went into a different school?" With every prohibitive response from the person behind the desk, I kept asking, "What if...?" "What about...?" "What would it take...?"

After three or four days of this, I finally found an advocate, someone much closer to my age—a student who worked in the admissions office as his student employment. "Yeah, you know, you're right," the younger man said. "That guy has a confirmed spot in the dorm. He's got a freshman schedule. He even has financial aid." One by one, I started chipping away at the barriers, none of which constituted a major issue but collectively looked rather daunting.

About a week after the semester started, I was officially a Georgetown student living in a dorm with enough financial aid to pay for my first semester plus books. When the second semester rolled around, I was still enrolled, but I had to secure more financial aid. I employed the same system and ended up with a suitable result. Using similar tactics over the next three years, I attended and graduated from Georgetown University without having been officially accepted and without paying a dime. I simply gathered up aid from students who had left the school for various reasons.

Years later, everyone who hears that story says basically the same thing: "That's impossible. You just can't do that." In my naïveté, it never occurred to me that it wouldn't work. Besides, I had no backup plan, other than going back to the pick and shovel.

GENIUS TALENT IN OUR DNA

I was nineteen when I pulled off my first free year at Georgetown. I didn't know anything about genius talent or the how and why behind what I was doing. I just knew there had to be a way to get into the university of my choice—that this situation was only *seemingly* impossible—and through a nonlinear, trial-and-error process, I figured it out as I went. By the end of my time in school, I even had a group of people in the Georgetown office quietly rooting for me, the underdog who was possibly succeeding against all protocol and against all odds. In a sense, my win was a win for the staff as well: they had fun helping me beat the system, knowing that they played a part in my success.

Years later I realized my actions gave evidence to my singular gift of genius talent—a talent that was embedded in my DNA without me even knowing it. Today I would state my genius talent like this:

> My genius talent is creating seemingly impossible outcomes, that address multiple and divergent agendas. I do this by creating one unifying game, by enrolling each of the participants, and then by continually altering the game and its rules so that everyone gets exactly what they came for.

Can you see how this talent could lead to some pretty amazing results in seemingly impossible situations? But how helpful would it be if I had to facilitate the building of a house? Or organize a community garage sale? Or design an accounting software program? Not very. I'm at my best when I take on a task that others consider impossible (and, hence, dismiss out of hand), and I have the freedom to figure it out—even better when I have the pressure of a short time frame to pull out a miracle. Oftentimes, I get the job because no one else sees it as attractive or even feasible. I get the lost causes. If you give me a project with a designated due date and prescribed series of logical steps, I'll be bored to death and I'll probably set the task aside or mess it up. That's the way genius talent works: in the appropriate context it's amazingly powerful, but it's irrelevant in situations that don't allow for its full expression.

Maybe you can relate. Perhaps you have requirements at work, like conducting peer reviews or completing quarterly expense reports, that have to get done but leave you bored and frustrated because they don't take advantage of your skills. Or maybe there are parts of household maintenance such as fixing leaky faucets, doing laundry, and mowing the lawn that drive you crazy, either because you hate doing them or you're not good at them or they simply suck up your whole Saturday.

What if situations like this weren't a problem anymore? What if you approached every area of life—work, home life, parenting, friendships, hobbies, volunteering—through the lens or pathway provided by your singular gift of genius talent? And what if that talent were already a constitutive part of who you are—in other words, what if you were born this way?

That's the purpose of this book: to help you discover your genius talent—the talent that's yours alone and that you may already be expressing without fully realizing it—and let it guide every area of your life.

THE CAVEAT AND IRONY OF GENIUS TALENT

If I showed you a suitcase with $1 million in it and you got to keep every penny for answering one question, you certainly would give your best effort. Here's the question I ask a lot: for $1 million, what is your singular gift of genius talent, the one contained in your DNA?

Nothing difficult. Nothing fancy. Just tell me what genius talent you received, different from every other human being on the planet—your one-in-a-billion talent, if you will. For $1 million, you certainly should be able to say this accurately.

However, most people shrug and say, "I have no idea."

That's the caveat: having a genius talent does not mean you know it and use it. That's also the irony: even though that talent is embedded in every cell of your body, you cannot state what it is clearly, let alone utilize it on a daily basis.

Call it dark humor.

THE PROCESS

When my partners and I initially started this talent discovery process in 2007, we walked people through a labor-intensive three-hour interview and then handed them a seven-page written assessment at completion. We found that even though we had spent hours uncovering their amazing talent, people walked away not really believing they possessed it and they never used the findings in the report. The breakthrough came two years later, when we stopped telling people their talent and allowed them to voice it back to us on their own. We started teasing out their ideas, repeating them back to the participants so they could hear the language and then put it into their own words. Once people started taking ownership of the language, they started living out their talents much more often. We have taken more than 8,000 people through this process with a 100 percent success rate. Everyone has a singular gift of genius talent; it's just a matter of uncovering and then articulating it in one's own language.

This book itself is evidence of my genius talent in action. For years I said this nonlinear discovery process could not be captured in a linear format, namely, a book; it seemed impossible to me. Then one day my personal coach said, "Aren't you the seemingly impossible guy? If this is impossible, then you are the one person on this planet who should be writing this book." He was right, and you now hold the evidence in your hands.

Many books have been written imploring people to connect with and find their highest talents. Duh! Who would not want to do that? This book is a do-it-yourself, how-to manual to get you there. It's not a theoretical discussion of gifts and talents; it's a strong call to action—actually, a mandate. You have a talent, and this book will help you uncover it, clearly articulate it, and put it to use.

If you're willing to invest the necessary time and energy, and if you're willing to follow the path provided in this book and in the accompanying online laboratory, you will come away with a beautiful and powerful statement of your genius talent. In addition, you'll learn how to own your talent and implement it in ways that improve your relationships, grow your income, and increase your passion, joy, and work satisfaction. Work will quickly begin to feel much more like play. As a good friend put it after having discovered and implemented his genius talent, "My Tuesdays now feel like Saturdays!"

Oliver Wendell Holmes once said, "Many people die with their music still in them." Don't let that be true of you.

The journey starts with mining for the greatness within.

PRO TIP

When you dive into the process itself, you might find yourself confused, lost, frustrated, and/or in need of more examples and explanation at various points along the way. Don't worry! Help is available on the companion website, where you'll find short video tutorials, pro tips, user feedback, learning partners, and more.

PART I

MINING FOR GREATNESS

In the first section, we will uncover patterns and themes that show up at your highest points of accomplishment, times when you have surpassed even your own expectations for performance. We will work primarily from the limbic brain, where we store every emotion and memory. The limbic brain has no language; it is neither linear nor logical. The prefrontal neocortex, on the other hand, is the seat of analysis, rational thought, language, and reason. Think of it this way: the limbic brain is the part of you that decided to buy a Hummer when you were supposed to buy a minivan, and the prefrontal neocortex justifies to your spouse why that decision was such a great move.

By tapping into the limbic brain, we receive an emotional, unpolished, and unedited feed from which we can tease out your genius talent. In mining, they call this raw material "ore."

This discovery process is challenging and is perhaps unlike anything you've done before. To help you navigate the steps as smoothly as possible, chapter 1 discusses eight keys to successfully navigating the discovery process and several practical "getting started" tasks. Chapter 2 covers important listening skills you will use throughout the process, and chapter 3 dives into the first stage of the process itself.

Throughout part I you'll find pro tips as well as prompts to check out the book's website, where you'll find a process flowchart and short videos that demonstrate the process in action. If you follow the commando squad model shown in this book, completing Part I will involve the amount of time it takes you to read chapters 1–3 plus two hours for a video call. At the end of that time, you'll have what you need to uncover your singular gift of genius talent.

Curious what finished genius talent statements look like? You'll find examples at the beginning of each chapter—statements that were formed by people just like you using the same discovery process you're about to begin.

When you finish part I, you'll be ready to move on to part II, which takes you through the process of uncovering your gift. At the end of part II, you'll have a powerful and beautiful statement of the unique gift you can offer to the world and, perhaps more importantly, to yourself. You'll also have your purpose on earth, or your *why*, which fuels your individual talent.

Are you ready to jump in?

Chapter 1

KEYS TO SUCCESS

"My unique genius is declaring compelling ideas that others bring into existence. I do this by getting really frustrated about a situation, by identifying the problem and addressing the limiting beliefs beneath it, and finally by creating a captivating challenge and surrounding myself with people capable of creating the new reality. I do this because I believe that there is no can't...only won't."

—BILL H., RICHMOND, VIRGINIA

THE OBJECTIVES

- Understand the recommendations and criteria for successfully completing the genius talent discovery process in an unhosted commando squad

- Decide whether the unhosted commando squad is the best method for you and if not, choose an alternative method such as hiring a coach

If you read the introduction to part I, you probably noticed chapter 1 contains background information. You may be tempted to skip it. Don't! Under penalty of severe physical pain, stick with it. After reading the next few pages, you will have a better idea of what's involved and be able to decide how you want to proceed. You may also want to review the process options discussed in the No-Nonsense, No BS Disclaimer before you waste time or get lost in a discovery method that's not right for you.

THE KEYS

If you read the No BS Disclaimer, then you know the most effective, low-cost approach described in this book requires you to work with one or two other people, preferably random strangers. If you're still trying to figure out if this option is for you, consider the following attitudes and mindsets we know contribute to a successful outcome in a commando squad. Ask yourself the following questions; your answers will help you determine which approach is best for you.

1. PLAY BY THE RULES

- Are you willing to meet and work with people you don't know? *Really*?
- Are you willing to follow directions and heed the pro tips you'll be given along the way?

- Are you willing to be a team player, or are you a ball hog? Be honest.

Being *willing* to play is the number one key to success. This process involves teamwork—as mentioned, it's nearly impossible to work your way through this book and get really clear results on your own. Are you willing to play with others and follow the guidelines? If not, you might get better results by hiring a coach to take you through the process privately in a one-on-one consultation, or by working with some colleagues and a paid facilitator.

2. SEEK BETTER FOR YOURSELF AND OTHERS

- Do you want to grow and learn?
- Do you like to grow and learn?
- Do you want family, friends, and coworkers to experience growth and improvement in their own lives?
- Do you want a better marriage, better friendships, better health?
- Do you want your work to feel like play?
- Do you want these things for others?

If you answer yes to these questions, you're a great fit for this discovery process in a commando squad.

3. HAVE AN ATTITUDE OF COLLABORATION

- Do you take as much pleasure in a team win as you do in an individual win?
- Do you enjoy helping someone else achieve their goal and get to where they want to be?
- Do you celebrate when you accomplish a goal or create a big win?

If you answered yes, then you're a good fit for this process in a commando squad. In fact, collaboration is at the heart of the genius talent discovery process. If you're only focused on your own self-improvement, this might not be the book for you; instead, you might want to hire a coach for a one-on-one experience.

4. APPRECIATE AND PARTNER WITH PEOPLE WHO ARE DIFFERENT FROM YOU

- Do you see the value of working with people who don't see the world the way you do?
- Do you like people on purpose, especially when they might not be your same demographic or share your same beliefs or values?

Having different perspectives and world views can be extremely beneficial in this discovery process. In fact, we've found that people get more accurate results in finding their genius talent when there's more, rather than less, diversity in the conversation. If you prefer working with people who are like you or if you want the privacy of your own worldview, a commando squad is probably not a great fit for you. Hire a private coach instead. Information on how to do that can be found at www.oneinabillionbook.com.

5. ASK FOR AND ACCEPT HELP

- Do you ask for help, or do you insist on doing everything yourself (even when you're failing)?
- More importantly, can you accept help when it's offered?

Chances are that you will be confused and possibly frustrated at different points in this process, and you will have opportunities to ask for help. There are many forms of assistance for you and your commando squad, and successful groups use them. If you're not good at asking for or accepting help, save yourself the headache of playing in a commando squad, as you and your teammates will invariably need help to successfully complete the process. In the genius discovery process, asking for and accepting help is a key to success and a strength, not a verdict of failure.

6. DON'T PARTNER WITH FRIENDS AND FAMILY

We mentioned this in the disclaimer, but just in case you missed it: working with people you don't know produces better results because you tend to lean into the process in an unbiased way. As counterintuitive as it may sound, running a clean process with people you don't know ranks far superior to running a biased process with people you do know. For accountability purposes, it can be helpful to go through the process at the same time as a friend or family member, but we recommend doing so in separate groups. After you discover and articulate your genius talent with your commando squad, you can share it with family and friends. As mentioned in the No BS Disclaimer, the quality of your talent statement will not be as high if you uncover it with friends and family.

7. FOLLOW THE DESIGNATED SEQUENCE

This point is related to the question of whether you are willing to follow directions. It is important to go through this book in the prescribed order and to work through the designated chunks—and only those chunks—in each video call. You will be given advanced notice of the chapters to review at one time and approximately how much time that will take. If you're not so strong in the direction-following department, or if you tend to invent your own path, hire a coach to work with you one-on-one or in a facilitated commando squad.

On the companion website, you will have opportunities to offer feedback on the process, and we will continually strive to make the process simpler and more effective. That said, what is presented has a track record of 8,000 successful genius talent discoveries. Follow it and succeed.

8. ENJOY THE JOURNEY

The process will be challenging, and you will stumble through it at times. Are you okay with that? Can you enjoy the journey even if it's not perfect? Do you have the ability to laugh at yourself a bit, give a fist pump, and move forward? If so, get ready to join a commando squad and start the ride!

WHAT'S NEXT?

You've read the No BS Disclaimer and the keys to success, and you've decided you're all in for the commando squad approach. Great! The next step is to go online and register so we can match you up with two people who have also decided to take the commando squad approach. Go to www.oneinabillionbook.com. You'll be asked to register your name, city and state, and photo. We promise not to sell any of your registration details. Feel funny about uploading a picture? Think of it this way: would you trust a partner you don't know if you don't know what he or she looks like? Probably not.

Once you register, we will match you with two partners,

and then send all three of you an email introduction. We try to match people in the same time zone so it is easier to coordinate video calls, but other than that, the matching process is essentially random.

PRO TIP

After you've learned who you're teamed up with, you might be tempted to Google them. Please don't! It's better to come into the first call not knowing what your partners do for a living. Some professions can create bias before you even begin—if you found out one person in your group is the head executioner for the state of California, would you form certain opinions? Likewise, we recommend that you don't tell your partners what you do. The introductory email to you and your two partners will have some tips on how to get to know each other, without going into detail about professions.

Some people approach getting to know an individual with an attitude of "impress me with the things I might like about you" rather than seeing the person as a valuable human being simply because she is breathing. In each video interaction, endeavor to find things to like about each person in your commando squad, rather than putting that person in a place of trying to impress you. Likewise, don't try to impress your partners; no need to tell them that you're a thought leader or you belong to Mensa or you graduated top of your class at MIT. As you'll discover, your genius talent most likely won't have much to do with IQ, yet it will still be envied by your partners who don't possess it.

Remember, we're discovering talent, not comparing professions, and we're not trying to establish our rank or aptitude. Seeing value in people for who they are, not what they do, is a fundamentally different way of relating to people. It's more inclusive and authentic, and what you discover is much more interesting. You discover what people are passionate about, and even if you're not interested in those events or hobbies, you can appreciate the enthusiasm the other person has. Appreciation of that passion makes us like the other person.

After you've met your team via email, the next step is to schedule your first call. Book a two-hour video conference using a Zoom video link (we have one for you on the portal). Make sure you choose a day and time when you can be in a quiet place without distractions for the entire two-hour call.

Your online registration gives you full access to additional content on our website: updated pro tips, videos, feedback from other successful commando squads, and other resources to help if you get stuck somewhere in the process. Each time your group meets, each person will log in to the website and follow the flowchart so you are ready to access these videos and other resources as you need them. The site will know where you are in the process so that appropriate help is available at each step.

Trying to complete the process while looking at the book would be clunky and very difficult. Think about a handbook for conducting a great first date: the handbook might be super informational, sure, but to enjoy the date itself, you cannot have your nose in a book when there's a delightful person sitting across from you—with his or her nose in the same book! The discovery process works the same way. Read the book, but when it comes time to play, shift over to the website, which is designed to be more fluid and allows you to focus on the people (virtually) in front of you.

Before you participate in your first call, read chapter 2 for key points on listening and note-taking. Grasping and following these tips will make all the difference in navigating your first call as smoothly and successfully as possible. It will still be challenging, but you will have the tools to collect the raw materials you need to help your partners uncover their genius talent.

PRO TIP

As mentioned, navigating this process requires a team; you can't do it with any degree of accuracy on your own. In teams of three, you will need an estimated ten hours to complete the whole process, which could potentially spread out over several months. At the end of that time you will have met two incredible people with whom you'll probably remain lifelong friends.

You have to ask yourself if you're willing to make that time commitment. If not, you can go through the process in two hours working one-on-one with one of our trained coaches. This option requires a fee, obviously, but you may decide the fee is worthwhile if you can achieve the same results in two hours instead of ten. The choice is yours. If you choose to hire us, go to www.oneinabillionbook.com, where you'll be guided to a code for a discount since you already purchased this book.

Chapter 2

———

ACTIVE LISTENING

"*My genius talent is creating the resources to change lives. I do this by expecting the extraordinary, by preparing myself for the next open door, and then by taking full advantage of every opportunity. I do this because fundamentally I believe blessings should be shared.*"

—LAURA P., SAN JOSE, CALIFORNIA

THE OBJECTIVE

Learn a specific manner of listening that will keep you and your partners engaged with one another and help you succeed more readily in the genius talent discovery process.

If you're still reading, one of two things is going on: you have either decided that a commando squad is for you and you're still learning all you can before you launch, or you're still not sure which option is quite right for discovering your genius talent. Either way, you'll definitely want to read this chapter before you get onto your first call with your commando squad or coach. This chapter discusses some of the key skills you'll need to employ throughout the process.

WHAT IS LISTENING?

Has your mother-in-law ever given you career advice? Because she's your mother-in-law, you're polite and you nod your head at the appropriate moments. But are you really listening? Probably not.

Real listening comes in two forms, based on whom you're serving. If I ask for directions, for example, I listen intently to the answer because I need the information to get from point A to point B. The person giving me directions is valuable to me at that moment, and I listen because it will serve me.

Listening in service to myself differs from listening in service to the Speaker. The latter is a specific kind of active listening and is probably something you've never done before. We often think of active listening as being engaged in the conversation through commenting, responding, and gathering information so that we can respond. That kind of listening actually serves the listener—the person preparing to respond. In the genius talent discovery process, however, listeners don't respond at all. They just listen intently and take notes on behalf of the Speaker. The act of listening really has nothing to do with the listeners; they just happen to have the ears to hear and the pen and paper to record the answers.

ACTIVE LISTENING TIPS

If you are working through this book in a group of three, you will have one Speaker and two listeners at any given time. Listening effectively is absolutely essential to gleaning information to help the Speaker uncover his or her talent.

When you play the listener role, you will be taking notes on what the Speaker is sharing. The following are listening tips specifically related to the note-taking you will be doing in service to your Speaker:

- Think of yourself as a court reporter or stenographer. You don't have an opinion on anything being shared, and if you do, it matters little. Your job is to write down the stated words without reaction, comment, or judgment.
- Think of your hand and pen as an extension of the Speaker's lips. As such, write down the exact words spoken—not a paraphrase or the words you might choose. For example, if the Speaker says, "I hit it out of the park," that's what you write—not "I hit a

home run." If the Speaker says, "I was devastated," write "devastated"—not "heartbroken" or "crushed." What comes from the Speaker's lips goes through the listener's hand and directly onto the paper without commentary, judgments, or questions. The listeners have no agenda of their own. They hear the words and write them down.

- Take notes in the first person. As you write, pretend you are the Speaker. Remember to keep bullet points brief, but if a key point involves pronouns, use I, me, my, and mine as appropriate.
- Take handwritten notes! Please, please do not use a computer, phone, tablet, or any other typing device. Your brain processes information differently when you're taking notes on a word processor. We want the hand-brain connection associated with handwritten notes.
- Take notes in bullet-point phrases. You won't have time to write full sentences, so just get the main exact words. For example, if the Speaker says, "When I was in seventh grade...," just write "seventh grade" and move on to the next bullet point. If someone says, "I tried out for the basketball team," write "basketball team." In a two- to three-minute story, you'll probably have ten to fifteen bullet points. See Figure 2.1 for a sample page of notes.
- Please do not polish, rewrite, clean up, or expand your notes after the call ends. If they look raw and unpol-

ished, you've done this step perfectly. We want the raw feed you initially wrote down. It's perfect. It's the ore that contains the precious metal needed.

- Don't share your notes with others. We've had people say to the others in their group, "I want to know what you wrote about me. Can you both send me the notes you took on me?" No. Seeing the notes won't help the Speaker in the genius talent discovery process. The notes are 99 percent ore from which we need to mine the 1 percent gold or silver that makes up the genius talent.

Julie
4th grade

- all white community
- year younger than other kids
- walk every day half mile to school
- arrive super early
- Stacey arrives early too, in blue camper
- Stacey's family lives in camper
- dad drops her off
- Stacey drinking from a thermos. "It's coffee"
- tell my Dad: "I know why Stacey has dark skin. She drinks coffee."
- Dad: "We don't treat people who drink coffee any differently."
- Stacey becomes best friend
- spends lots of time at our home
- Mom and Dad treat Stacey like family

MSFT
35(ish)

- my meeting, with other Team Leaders
- team budget cutting meeting: "We need to be more efficient."
- windowless conf room, fluorescent lighting
- "We've got this data. We've got that data…."
- Michael B is quiet
- Michael only participant to turn to speakers to listen
- MB on low end of experience and authority
- I notice how differently MB listens and pays attention
- MB hesitant to speak or give opinions
- Me: "I'm interested in what you think."
- MB outlines the inefficiencies that he sees
- no one else sees this
- No layoffs needed—only changes in budgets

Libby	-	Libby junior at Oregon - Bio-Chem major
(daughter)	-	met friends last night - Wild Duck Cafe
	-	finals done that day
	-	her friends come to dinner
	-	Maddie first to arrive with Libby
	-	Maddie obviously not bio-chem major. Mocks labs and flasks
	-	'grounding force'
	-	'intellectual zen' - black circular glasses - delightful
	-	Nikki and PJ (boy) - couple arrive
	-	PJ smartest person I've ever met w/sharp wit
	-	Nikki half Japanese/half white with red dyed hair - beautiful
	-	Nikki - high IQ, high EQ
	-	Dan is missing. Engineering major
	-	Dan "tumbles" into restaurant - low key guy
	-	I notice who they are each as individuals
	-	I notice how they all contribute to cool, nerdy, comfortable group
	-	Notice how to minimize input from some, and draw out input from others
	-	finals are done, and all will travel to Seattle for 4 days together at my house before going to their own homes
	-	love that they are happy and relaxed together at my home
	-	they take over the whole place for 4 fun days
	-	love that Libby has this great group of friends

Sample bullet point notes

TIME TO LISTEN

Now you've met your partners, at least via email, and you've learned a little more about how the process works and the time involved if you proceed in your group of three. Before you move on to the next chapter, do a little introspection and confirm that you still want to work through the discovery process with two strangers. It does get clunky and it could be potentially frustrating at times. Are you willing to stick with it for however long it takes? If you opt out halfway through because you decide it's too hard or you don't like your partners or it's taking too long or whatever, you'll leave your partners hanging. Better to decide now, before your first call.

The quality of the mining for genius stands in direct proportion to the quality of your listening. Are you ready to be in full service to your partners?

PLAN AHEAD

Here's a preview of how much time you'll spend in each part of the first video call. The specific instructions for each part are covered in chapter 3. The first call will last around two hours. Before you start the call, discuss whether you will all be able to stay on past the two hours in order to finish. Especially for the first call, it's important to not have someone leave early, so pad your schedules. Perhaps you can make sure you have two and a half hours free. You most likely will not need that much time, but better to finish early, than to have to split your call.

The first call should be broken up approximately as follows:

- Thirty minutes: introductions, deciding who will play which role, deciding who will go first.

- Thirty minutes: first person goes through the process.

- Twenty minutes: second person goes through the process.

- Twenty minutes: third person goes through the process.

Chapter 3

GATHERING RAW MEMORIES

"My genius talent is creating seemingly impossible outcomes that address multiple and divergent agendas. I do this by designing one unifying game, by enrolling each participant, and then by continually altering the rules and the outcomes so that everyone gets exactly what they came for. I do this because I believe when we play boldly together, everyone wins big."

—JOHN H., SAN JOSE, CALIFORNIA

THE OBJECTIVE

Follow the process and script exactly as laid out in this chapter to gather stories from the limbic brain that will form the basis for constructing a genius talent statement.

How do we craft a genius talent statement like the ones you see at the beginning of each chapter—equal parts beauty and power? The foundation of your genius talent statement comes from the raw materials that show up in the form of repeated patterns when you're performing at peak level. In the introduction I shared the story of how I got into Georgetown. I've also successfully negotiated a hostage negotiation. The common theme in these stories is that when I'm in high performance, usually with pressure to act, seemingly impossible outcomes appear for both myself and those around me.

This chapter describes the process of mining for greatness—connecting with emotions and memories that reveal glimpses of your genius talent. To do so, you have to start off in the right frame of mind.

RELAXING THE SPEAKER

Have you ever noticed that when people are relaxed and let their guard down, they become a little more vulnerable and authentic, and you gain a clearer path to who they are? You get a window into people's true selves when they relax, when the front they might sometimes hide behind comes down. When people are relaxed and comfortable, we see a different and perhaps more authentic version than if they are posturing, pretending, or feeling uptight.

When people let their hair down a little, whether because they've had a couple beers or because they're feeling reflective, it's a beautiful moment. If you're hanging out with your mom, for example, and you both feel relaxed, Mom might confide that she and your dad struggled a few years back, and they saw a counselor to fix their marriage—something you never suspected or saw on your own.

Conversely, when someone has her guard up, an invisible barrier prevents others from getting to know her fully. I do it, too. In certain situations, there is only so much I am willing to show. This is simply a protection mechanism, and we all have a sense of when to ratchet that up. This protective instinct will not help in the section we take on now.

In this discovery process, relaxing the Speaker properly is even more important than proper listening and note-taking. If the Speaker is relaxed, stories flow naturally and provide an unedited raw feed from which to construct the talent statement. If the Speaker is not relaxed, however, he will be worried about looking good in front of his partners and stories will come out in a sanitized, self-edited, or inauthentic manner. The ore in this case yields only cubic zirconium, not a real diamond.

PREPARATION

Once you all join the first video call, you have a few preliminary tasks before you start mining for greatness:

Meet and Greet

This is the first time you've actually met your partners "face to face." Allow ten minutes for each person to introduce himself. Remember the pro tip from chapter 1: ask your partners about hobbies, family, volunteer work, and other areas of their life rather than what they do for a living. Check the website for a few suggestions to make this meet and greet more fun.

Decide Roles

As mentioned, during each part of the process, one person will be speaking and two people will be listening. The Speaker, as we'll call this person, is the individual who is sharing; in any given session, the group is helping the Speaker uncover his talent. The listeners are both responsible for listening in service to the Speaker and taking careful notes. In addition, one listener in each session will lead the conversation; we'll call this person the Moderator. The other listener will be the primary listener and notetaker; we'll call this person the Scribe. You'll rotate roles at different points in the discovery process so that everyone has a chance to be Speaker, Moderator, and Scribe. The exact functions for each role show up more fully online.

There are a number of ways to decide who will be the first Speaker. Play rock, paper, scissors or ask a question like, "Who was born closest to Denver?" After the Speaker is determined, flip a coin or pick another random method to decide who will be the Scribe and who will be the Moderator. If you have a strong sense of which role you might do well in (remember, you are serving your partners here), volunteer for it.

One strong suggestion: it's more efficient to have the same Moderator for the first two Speakers. The first Speaker takes the longest anyway, so you can speed the process for the second Speaker by having a Moderator who is already familiar with the role. It's also more efficient to use a random rock, paper, scissors method to determine roles rather than have a long discussion.

Log On

At the beginning of each call, all three members of your commando squad should log on to the web portal and check the role they will be taking for that session. This way you will have videos and additional pro tips easily accessible if you get stuck, and you will have a personalized experience based on the role you're taking during that session.

Systems Check

The last preparation step is to make sure you and your space are ready for an uninterrupted two-hour call. What do we mean by "uninterrupted"? Good question. Here's a comparison of what you may think of as uninterrupted and what we actually mean:

WHAT YOU MIGHT THINK	WHAT WE MEAN
phone on vibrate	phone turned *off* and locked in the sealed bomb shelter in your backyard
multiple browser windows minimized	close all applications, especially those that "ding" when an email or text arrives
dog downstairs with the kids and spouse	dog, kids, spouse out of the house
in a conference room at work	at home alone
enough time allotted for call	extra thirty minutes allotted for call

Remember, as a listener you are in service to your partners. If your phone vibrates or the dog barks or if someone walks into the conference room and starts asking you questions, you'll feel terrible for ruining your commando squad partner's outcome. Imagine how you might feel if one of your partners damaged your process.

Here are a few more tips for setting up yourself and your space for success. These tips help you play the role of active listener in service to your Speaker:

1. Scribe: Mute your computer microphone when the

Moderator starts reading the script. You don't want to accidentally knock your desk or thump down a coffee cup or make any kind of noise that will distract the Speaker or bring him out of his relaxed state.

2. Scribe and Moderator: Be as physically still as possible. Remember this is a video conference, so your partners can see what you're doing. Even though the Speaker will have his eyes closed at times, he can still sense motion. If you are the Scribe, you'll be taking notes, so your hand will be moving, but stay in your seat. Each person needs your full attention on this first call; wait to stretch or grab your coffee cup in between speakers.

3. Everyone: Turn your phone off! Don't just set it to vibrate; turn the sound all the way off. Better yet, put it in Airplane Mode. Even on vibrate, the phone still makes a noise that can distract the Speaker and take him out of the moment.

4. Everyone: Close the windows and doors to block out ambient noise: barking dogs, UPS deliveries, ambulances, trash trucks, landscapers, and so on.

5. Everyone: Eat before you start the call. You don't want to be distracted by hunger pangs, and you definitely should not be eating during the call.

6. Everyone: Bring a beverage that relaxes you: a cup of tea, a soft drink, a glass of water; whatever puts you into your comfort zone.

7. Everyone: Be influence free: no alcohol or drugs

before or during the process. This process is not enhanced in the slightest by outside influences.

This is a dynamic process and we're always making improvements. If you want the latest script, along with tips, check the website.

THE SCRIPT

After everyone is settled into their chairs with their comforting beverage of choice, it's time to begin the relaxation process. As the Moderator reads the following script, the Speaker allows himself to be taken through the process. The Scribe will sit quietly for this part of the process but will have an active role shortly. Remember, all three members of your commando squad take turns to go through the same process on the first call.

While reading the script, the Moderator should take the vocal tone and slow pace one would use to read a bedtime story to a small child. She should speak very softly, slowly, and calmly, with the vocal tonality that would help a child relax. Tone alone can help relax the Speaker—or keep him tense.

Throughout the book, the script portion will be indented and any related explanation will be placed in brackets.

Are you ready? For the next twenty minutes (until the first Speaker has been taken through the relaxation process), the Moderator should use her bedtime story voice and cadence.

Okay, this next part will take about twenty minutes. Just relax, follow simple instructions, and enjoy the process.

First, let's check your physical setup. It's best if you're sitting in a straight-backed chair. Sit so that your hips, your knees, and your ankles are all at ninety-degree angles and your feet are firmly on the floor. Place your hands on your thighs, with your palms up or palms down.

Unless it makes you dizzy, gently close your eyes and keep them closed.

You've probably heard the terms *yoga breaths* or *cleansing breaths*. Some people call them deep breaths. Through your belly button—not your lungs—inhale and slowly count one, two, three. Then exhale and slowly count one, two, three. Then inhale and exhale. Continue this process of *long*, slow breaths in and *long*, slow breaths out. Focus on slowing down and elongating your breaths.

[Pause and allow the Speaker to take a few breaths in silence. He is relaxing, even if you are dying a bit inside.]

Now imagine you've got a wire thread tied to the top of

your head, and it's gently pulling you towards the ceiling. As it does, it elongates and straightens your spine. Your shoulders tend to naturally drop as you lengthen your spine.

[Again, pause for a few seconds.]

Inhale, long and slow; exhale, long and slow.

Now I'd like to transport you to the big island of Hawaii. You're on a beautiful beach at Mauna Kea. It's a perfect day, the midmorning sun warms the sand as you walk toward the ocean. The warm air caresses your skin. The water is imminently swimmable, clear, and inviting—the perfect temperature.

While you're on the beach, you notice, a short distance down the rocky shoreline, what looks like a lava outcropping. You decide to grab a snorkel, mask, and fins and swim out to explore. As you swim toward the lava outcropping, you see a couple of sea turtles and many kinds of colorful fish. The lava outcropping is only 250 yards away, and you have a delightful swim.

When you reach the backside of the rock outcropping, you notice a spot where you can stand waist-deep in the ocean, under a gentle waterfall that flows through the lava outcropping. Allow the waterfall to flow over your head, down your neck, and over your shoulders. As it does, allow the water to take away any present concerns you might have. Let the cascading water relax you completely.

[Pause]

Can you find yourself in the waterfall?

[Wait for an answer, often just a nod, and then pause again.]

Are you relaxed?

[Wait for an answer—again, often a nod, as the person is enjoying the waterfall.]

The Moderator shouldn't rush the Speaker after asking, "Can you find yourself in the waterfall?" and "Are you relaxed?" It's easy to freak out at the silence. The website has a timer to give a sense of how long the pauses should be; the Moderator should click it as soon as he asks, "Can you find yourself in the waterfall?" and not talk again until the time is up.

If you're a listener, waiting in silence and watching the Speaker sit with his eyes closed may drive your nervous system crazy. You may be tempted to jump in after a few seconds of quiet. Please don't! If you do, you will pull the Speaker out of the relaxed state he's entered. Give the Speaker at least thirty seconds to enjoy the waterfall.

Wouldn't you want to enjoy a gentle, warm cascading waterfall over your head, neck, and shoulders? Allow your Speaker the same pleasure. Consider this: You cannot mess up a pause by having it be too long. You can mess up the experience if you rush the pause that is relaxing the Speaker. Take your time!

If the Moderator asks, "Can you find yourself in the waterfall?" and the Speaker says, "I'm still getting there," then the Speaker is still in his head; he's not yet relaxed. If the Speaker says something like this, the Moderator should pause for at least fifteen seconds. Once the Speaker is there, let him enjoy the experience. Don't rush him out of the waterfall. Relaxation correlates directly to the success of mining for greatness.

If the Speaker is fully relaxed and immersed in the experience of the waterfall, his answer to the question "Are you relaxed?" will come out softly, barely a whisper. Some people don't even speak; they just nod their head. That's perfect!

If the first Speaker can't get relaxed, it's okay to switch roles. If someone has come straight from a stressful conference or just received a call that his kid is sick at daycare, that person might have a harder time finding himself under the waterfall. There's no sense in proceeding if the Speaker isn't relaxed. Trying to force relaxation is like trying to calm a screaming baby by yelling "Quiet down!" Instead, switch roles and let someone else be the Speaker.

EVOKING STORIES

After the Speaker is relaxed, the Moderator continues reading the script in a soft, calming voice. During this section, the Scribe is the primary notetaker, while the Moderator reads and takes notes. Remember, listeners: your notes should be handwritten bullet points in first person. Use the Speaker's exact word choice for key ideas. Your notes are an integral part of the genius talent discovery process, so listen carefully and let your hand be an extension of the Speaker's mouth.

THE SCRIPT

The script picks up once the Speaker is relaxing in the waterfall. In the call you will move seamlessly from relaxation into evoking stories. The sections are separated in the book for explanation only. The end of the previous script is included here so you can see how it flows:

Can you find yourself in the waterfall?

[Wait for an answer, often just a nod, and then pause again.]

Are you relaxed?

[Wait for an answer—again, often a nod, as the person is enjoying the waterfall.]

Just relax there for a moment.

[Wait before continuing.]

Great. Here's what I'd like you to do now. I want you to go back as far as you can when you were a young child and connect with an incredible sense of safety—a place or an atmosphere where you felt totally carefree, where you felt loved, where you could do anything you wanted. Maybe your basement was set up with a play area, and you would go down there and get lost in your toys. Or maybe you had a treehouse. Maybe you loved hanging out at Grandma's house at the holidays. Or maybe your family had a vacation spot you visited every year and when you arrived, it felt like a homecoming. Connect with a strong sense of being carefree, totally safe and loved.

After the Moderator gives the example, he should pause for five to ten seconds while the person connects with the emotion. It might take longer because the Speaker has probably never been asked that question. Then, the Moderator continues quietly:

Did you have a place like this when you were younger?

The Moderator should wait as long as it takes for the

person to say yes; then continue quietly, calmly, slowly. Note: people who had a rough childhood will often use the phrase, "I can't think of one" or "I'm trying to remember one." This may simply mean they did not have a safe place as a young child. The Moderator should note the Speaker's tone of voice. If he uses a normal volume and cadence, chances are he never got relaxed. Not finding a place can make the Speaker feel like he is doing the process wrong, which takes him into his prefrontal neocortex. Not ideal. The Moderator should lead the Speaker back into the waterfall and simply skip the childhood memory once he relaxes again.

When the Speaker is ready to proceed, the Moderator should move on to the next part of the script:

> Great. Here's what I'd like you to do now. I'd like you to relive and reexperience that carefree moment using your five senses. Be there again, as if it were today. Were you indoors or outdoors? Was it a specific time of year? Were you by yourself or with your siblings or friends? What did it smell like? What sounds did you hear? What sounds were present?
>
> Here's what I want you to do. I just want you to be in that place in a sensory mode. Relive it and enjoy it.

The Moderator should let the person sit in that space for fifteen or twenty seconds, and then continue.

Okay. This is probably the most important instruction I will give you: I'd like you to gently, gently release yourself from that landscape.

[Short pause.]

Now, I'd like you to move forward in time to what I'll call junior high: seventh, eighth, or ninth grade when you were twelve, thirteen, or fourteen years old. I'd like you to connect with an incredibly high sense of achievement or accomplishment for something you were able to pull off. Maybe it was an event or a school project. Maybe it was something in sports or in scouting or something you did in the neighborhood. Something you did on your own in a public venue or in the privacy of your family.

To be clear, this is not where your parents said, "We're really proud of you." Or where your teacher said, "Nice job on that science project." This is something where you said, "I can't believe I pulled that off."

Again, the Moderator should pause for a couple seconds to let the person connect with a memory and then ask,

Did you have an episode or accomplishment like that around this time period?

Most people will say, "Yeah, I think so," because they're

not sure if they've connected with the "right" thing or if they have the right story to tell. After the person responds, the Moderator continues:

> Great. What I'd like you to do is to set the stage for us, and relive and retell that story in the first person, as if it were happening right now.

When the Speaker starts talking, the listeners—both the Scribe and the Moderator—start taking bullet points as discussed in chapter 2. Don't interrupt the Speaker or leave your chair. You are now actively listening in service to the Speaker, and your only task is taking down the key words and ideas as bullet points. Most importantly, do not ask clarifying questions, even if they seem like they might help the story.

As soon as the Speaker stops, the Moderator says,

> Great story. Thank you for sharing. Take a couple more deep breaths. Now I'd like you to move forward in time, perhaps to high school or when you were out of school, and connect with another tremendous sense of personal achievement or accomplishment for something you were able to pull off.

The Moderator should pause for a couple of seconds to let the person connect with a memory. By watching the

Speaker's face on the video, the Moderator can often tell if the Speaker has connected with something. If it's not obvious, the Moderator should wait a little longer. The key is to not pressure the Speaker; let him confirm or acknowledge that he has a memory to share. Connecting with the second and third stories is often easier than the first, as the Speaker gets the hang of the exercise.

Then the Moderator asks,

> Did you have something like that around this time period? Great. What I'd like you to do again is set the stage for me. Relive and retell that story in the first person, as if it were happening right now.

And then the Speaker is off, sharing his second story and the listeners are taking bullet point notes in service to the Speaker.

When the Speaker finishes, the Moderator says,

> Great. Thank you for sharing that story. Take a couple of deep breaths. Now you're going to move forward in time, perhaps to adulthood, and connect with another high sense of achievement.

After pausing and watching the Speaker's reaction, the Moderator asks,

Did you have something like that around this time period? Great. What I'd like you to do, again in a sensory experience, is set the stage for me. Relive and retell that story in the first person.

As the Speaker shares his third story, the Scribe and Moderator again take notes.

The Moderator takes the Speaker through the connection process one more time, again by gently asking if he has another story he'd like to share. The goal is to end up with at least three stories from each Speaker, but ideally four; the more, the better in terms of having additional reference points in the next section.

When the Speaker is done, the Moderator says,

> Terrific! Take a couple deep breaths. Slowly open your eyes. You did a great job. You are now done with part I.

And then your commando squad switches roles so someone else can go through the process. As suggested, you might keep the same Moderator since the person is already familiar with the script. Or you can rotate; that's up to your group.

The Moderator takes the new Speaker all the way through the process, starting with the relaxation script. Once the person is relaxed, the Moderator proceeds through the evoking stories section of the script. When the Speaker is sharing stories, both listeners again capture the key words and emotions in bullet points. Once the second Speaker has connected with and shared at least three experiences of high achievement, person number three is the Speaker and one of his partners reads the script following the same format.

As soon as all three team members have gone through the process, your group is done with part I and that's the end of your first video call. Even if you have time left over, please do not begin part II.

HINTS FOR THE MODERATOR AND SCRIBE

Here are some tricks we've found helpful as we lead people through the evoking stories phase:

- When the Moderator asks, "Have you found a place where you felt completely carefree?" most people will say, "Yeah, I think so." They aren't sure because they're not exactly sure what they're supposed to find. If the person can connect with the emotion called carefree, he can also connect with an emotion called anger and with love. This means the person is in his limbic brain. The Moderator shouldn't ask for any specifics, other than to find a place where the

Speaker feels carefree. We don't even want the person to describe the place; just to experience the feeling of being carefree there. This small child experience is really just practice and quality control, to see if the Speaker really is relaxed. We do not need the small child story.

- For transitioning after the Speaker's first story: Keep it simple and short. Don't say something like, "Wow, I loved that story. That was amazing." Instead, simply acknowledge the story is finished and move on as neutrally as possible. The more you talk to the Speaker at this point, the more likely he is to slip back into the prefrontal neocortex, so keep it short and to the point, still using your read-a-bedtime-story-to-a-child voice.

- Some people were miserable in junior high school or high school, because they were fat or had pimples or their family moved several times, so they had no friends. They most likely won't have high-achievement junior high and high school stories. No problem at all! No need to torture people by demanding they produce a story from high school; just move forward in time. In the end, the stories can come from any period of a person's life, and they do not even have to be in chronological order.

AVOID AT ALL COSTS

As mentioned, mining for greatness is the foundation of

this process. The rest of the steps hinge on the Speaker being able to tap into the limbic brain, connect emotionally with key stories, and share a raw feed that's recorded by the listeners. Because the listening skill is so different, some of you might worry about doing it wrong and messing up the process for your partners. If you feel like you've put your full effort toward serving your Speaker, you're probably fine. In fact, there are very few ways you can truly blow it. If you avoid the following no-nos at all costs, you'll be fine.

DON'T PLAY THERAPIST!

When the Speaker finishes a story, the listeners might be tempted to ask follow-on questions, whether because they're fascinated and curious or they think the person could add more details. Don't do it. The person's story is enough. Once the listeners start asking questions, they bring the Speaker out of the limbic brain and back into the neocortex; now the Speaker is *remembering* and analyzing instead of connecting with emotions, and the raw feed gets interrupted.

The Scribe and Moderator must trust the Speaker told the story the way he wanted to tell it. Some people tell thin stories; in other words, they don't have many details. In these cases, listeners are often tempted to ask follow-on questions. As you will learn in chapter 4, genius talents are gleaned from patterns, and patterns come from emotion—not details. Asking follow-on questions is a social activity we engage in at parties, but what you're engaged in here is different. The best service to the Speaker is to follow the process. Remember the first key to success: be willing to play with others and follow the designated guidelines.

DON'T RESCUE THE SPEAKER (IN OTHER WORDS, SHUT YOUR DAMN MOUTH!)

This is a crucial point. If the Speaker is properly relaxed and fully immersed in the limbic brain, he can become very emotional. That's okay; the listeners should not rescue him from the experience. Remember, the person is at home, he isn't in any danger, and you and your partner aren't doing any damage to the person. It's just emotion, nothing more. Your empathy, especially spoken, hurts rather than helps the process. Think of tears as tears of joy, since the person is telling an achievement story. Do not interrupt or offer to take a break. Just stay with the Speaker, especially if he needs to pause and gather himself for a moment.

Listeners, don't ask if the Speaker needs a break; this will only interrupt the flow and pull the person out of the limbic brain. The most empathetic thing you can do as a listener, the highest service you can have for your Speaker, is to keep your damn mouth shut. Let him be emotional. Rescuing the Speaker can have horrendous results in terms of mining for the raw materials for constructing one's genius talent. The Speaker has to be relaxed again, and because he has been drawn out of the limbic brain, the story he had been telling is useless.

DON'T AD-LIB

When you are the Moderator, don't add or omit words, summarize, or paraphrase the script. There's a reason the script is written the way it is. We want to ease the Speaker into the water and under the waterfall. We want to do it gently and take our time getting there, rather than abruptly plunge him in with statements like, "You're at the beach. It's a beautiful day. The ocean is here. Go on, get in!"

You don't make the story better with ad-libs; you wreck the process and interrupt the flow. We don't really care if we take the Speaker to Hawaii or Bermuda; the whole point is to get the person to relax. We don't even care about the waterfall, really. It's just a way to relax the Speaker and get him out of his head. At the same time, relaxing the Speaker should not take twenty minutes. This isn't guided meditation, and it certainly isn't hypnosis; we're doing genius discovery. Just follow the script and focus on your vocal tonality and slow, relaxing cadence.

WRAP-UP

Congratulations! You finished part I. You have mined for greatness and now have a set of stories for each person in your commando squad. If you have any questions at this point, check the FAQ section for part I on the website.

You should end your call here and start part II on your next call. Part II is a longer process and will be tackled over three to four separate calls. Store your notes in a safe place and be sure to bring them with you to the next call. Remember not to share your notes with the Speaker. That hurts, rather than helps, his genius talent discovery.

Do you feel like you've met people in a different way than you've met anyone else in your life? Why not keep the momentum going? Schedule your next call as soon as possible so you can continue the progress and continue the fun.

Once again, well done! You have acted in service to your partners, and you have connected with your own emotional moments. You're about 15 percent done with the process at this point. You are on to the next step of the journey.

ARTICULATING BEAUTY AND POWER

Congratulations! You now have the raw materials from which you can create a three-part genius statement. We'll discuss the three parts in more detail, but for now we'll call them your *what* (the talent you received), your *how* (how you demonstrate or bring forth that talent, step by step), and your *why* (your purpose in life, or why you're on this planet).

Part II is the meat of the genius discovery process and will take on a completely different form than part I. You'll decide who goes first and then work your way through chapters 4 through 8 one person at a time. In part I, all three members of the commando squad went through the process in one call, but that's not the case for part II. It will take around two hours to take each person through chapters 4 through 8, and possibly a bit longer for the first person.

Whereas part I had to be done all at once, part II does not; you can stop between chapters and continue on another call, if necessary. The first person will be the most challenging because it's your first time going through this process. You might even consider hiring a guide for the first person, to make the process go more smoothly, to cut down on potential frustration, and to get your questions answered on the spot. After that, you will be better equipped to handle the second and third person on your own during the next two calls.

In part I you used the limbic part of your brain to generate a raw emotional feed of stories. In part II you will use the prefrontal neocortex to analyze that raw feed and look for recurring patterns and themes. You will sift through the iron ore, so to speak, looking for the hidden and valuable gems. The prefrontal neocortex provides the analytical and language skills to identify themes, make connections, and verbalize what you discover. The neocortex also enables you to wordsmith those connections into a polished genius statement that is roughly equal parts beauty and power. *Listening* in a specific manner mattered in part I. In part II, *language* is what matters—specifically language that appeals to you.

Wondering what finished genius statements look like? You've seen a few at the beginning of chapters 1, 2, and 3. You can also check out the appendix, where you'll find more genius statements that illustrate what we mean by equal parts beauty and power. By the end of part II, you'll have your own.

PLAN AHEAD

Part II will involve approximately three two-hour video calls. Here's what you'll cover on each call:

- Call 2: First participant goes through part II

- Call 3: Second participant goes through part II

- Call 4: Third participant goes through part II

You will feel a great sense of accomplishment after uncovering and articulating each person's genius talent statement, as the process is most likely not like anything you have done before. Have fun!

Chapter 4

———

FINDING THEMES

"My genius talent is instigating adventures. I do this by lead-ing with infectious enthusiasm, by paying attention to what inspires other people, by recognizing potential adventures, and then by accepting whatever shows up along the way. I do this because happiness should be shared."

—RACHEL M., PORTLAND, OREGON

THE OBJECTIVE

Recognize patterns and themes associated with episodes of peak performance as a key step in forming a genius talent statement.

So, you have your three or four stories. What now? The steps in this chapter will guide you to find patterns and themes in your stories, then tease them out into key phrases and clauses that will fill out the genius talent framework. In doing this, step-by-step, you and your teammates will discover your *what*—your singular gift of talent. Finding themes is the key first step that makes the process flow.

Let's get started!

GET READY

On your second call, your first task will be to figure out who goes first: who is going to be the guinea pig or crash test dummy for this challenging yet rewarding process. You can again do something random, like who has the next birthday, or you can try a method like Think-Feel-Know.

Thinkers, feelers, and knowers all have different communication and decision-making styles. One isn't better than the others; they're simply different. We can all function in any of the three communication modes, but we also have a predominant or default mode. See if you can identify with one of the following descriptions as your primary mode of communicating:

- *Thinkers* look at an executive summary and say, "Thank God there are fifty pages of analytical research," and they read every page because they need to understand all the data before they move forward. They ask lots of questions and give lots of details in their answers. They are quite thorough. When you go out to dinner with a group of friends, the thinker is the one who wants to know the vegan options as well as the daily specials, and whether the special can be ordered without olives, how spicy the sauce is, and whether he can substitute rice for the mashed potatoes.
- *Knowers* skim the bullet points on the executive summary. They don't look at data, research, charts, or graphs because they don't need it; they're knowers. They already have a pretty good idea what they want to do, without getting bogged down in superfluous detail. At a restaurant, a knower sits down and, without looking at the menu, orders the biggest burrito available with the hottest sauce available. She knows what she wants and doesn't like being burdened by a million menu options. After all, it's a Mexican restaurant, so there's really only one good option.

- *Feelers* are a hybrid between thinkers and knowers. They read the executive summary, but not the additional fifty pages of data. They will read the highlights and then look at the visuals: pictures, graphs, colors, and charts. They love to use analogies, metaphors, and stories to illustrate their point. They work well from making "gut" decisions. When a feeler goes out to dinner, he watches the food trays being delivered to nearby tables and then tells the server he wants what the lady in the red dress is having because it looks and smells delicious. A feeler makes a sensory decision rather than an overly researched one.

Thinkers, knowers, and feelers will also approach this genius discovery process differently. If you use this method to determine who will go first, we suggest starting with the feeler or knower in your group. They will tend to move quicker in their responses.

After you figure out who goes first, decide who will be the Moderator. This person will read the script and any directions that need to be followed. The third person will be the Scribe—the primary notetaker. All three people should be logged into the website, but the Scribe will most likely be the one to check the website for tips or videos if you need help. The Moderator and the Scribe will work much more as partners in service to the Speaker from here forward, as part II is a robust discussion, rather than a linear process.

All three members of your commando squad should have their bullet point notes from the first call; you really can't proceed if you don't have both sets of notes for at least one of the three people on your team.

Once you're all seated with your notes and signed in to the website, it's time to dive in to the next step: finding patterns. Once again, the two listeners will be taking handwritten bullet point notes in first person using the exact words spoken by the Speaker. Remember: the listeners' hands and pens are an extension of the Speaker's lips.

SUGGEST THEMES

The Moderator starts by asking the Speaker,

> Did any of the three stories you told surprise you, as in "I don't think I have ever told that story before"?

This is a simple quality control check. Surprise stories confirm the person was indeed in the limbic part of the brain, and as a result, we probably mined fruitful ore, if you will. But not to worry if the Speaker isn't surprised; she can succeed in finding her talent either way.

After the Speaker responds, the Moderator continues:

> We realize you were telling the stories and focusing on

them. You did a great job. This is a bit of an unfair ask, but now that you have told your stories, were you able to notice any common or recurring themes or patterns running through all of them?

If the Speaker doesn't remember all three stories she shared, the other two team members can remind her of the topics, but not the details. For example, one of the listeners might say, "Oh, it was the science fair, the baseball game, and the birth of your first child." Then the Moderator can ask the question again about whether the Speaker noticed any recurring themes.

Let the Speaker think through her stories and offer up themes until she can't think of any more; that will often take two to three minutes. Oftentimes, the Speaker will have none. The listeners' job was to notice themes, not the Speaker's.

As the Speaker shares patterns, the listeners take bullet point notes and keep their mouths shut. More often than not, the themes that the Speaker offers are pretty obvious, like "I was the underdog" or "Overcoming a big obstacle." If the Speaker did not notice any patterns or themes (which is quite common), then simply move ahead.

Once the Speaker is finished, each listener will have a chance to share themes and patterns they noticed. The

Scribe and Moderator are offering *possibilities*; these patterns are not set in stone. The Speaker needs to be willing to hear what the others say, but more importantly, the listeners can't be adamant about the "rightness" of the patterns they observed. They should avoid the temptation to suggest a theme and then point out how it appears in each story; simply state the perceived pattern. If you end up with two or three themes, you're doing great.

Figure 4.1 illustrates patterns that one listener noticed in Julie's stories. The notes shown are the same as those in Figure 2.1, with the possible themes circled. Notice that often, the strongest themes do not show up in exact words, but in trends or unspoken attributes or actions.

Julie   -   all white community
4th grade   -   year younger than other kids
             -    walk every day half mile to school
             -    arrive super early
             -    Stacey arrives early too, in blue camper
             -    Stacey's family lives in camper
             -    dad drops her off
             -    Stacey drinking from a thermos. "It's coffee"
             -    tell my Dad: "I know why Stacey has dark skin. She drinks coffee."
             -    Dad: "We don't treat people who drink coffee any differently."
             -    Stacey becomes best friend
             -    spends lots of time at our home
             -    Mom and Dad treat Stacey like family

MSFT   -   my meeting, with other Team Leaders
35(ish) -   team budget cutting meeting: "We need to be more efficient."
             -    windowless conf room, fluorescent lighting
             -    "We've got this data. We've got that data…."
             -    Michael B is quiet
             -    Michael only participant to turn to speakers to listen
             -    MB on low end of experience and authority
             -    I notice how differently MB listens and pays attention
             -    MB hesitant to speak or give opinions
             -    Me: "I'm interested in what you think."
             -    MB outlines the inefficiencies that he sees
             -    no one else sees this
             -    No layoffs needed—only changes in budgets

```
Libby           -    Libby junior at Oregon - Bio-Chem major
(daughter)      -    met friends last night - Wild Duck Cafe
                -    finals done that day
                -    her friends come to dinner
                -    Maddie first to arrive with Libby
                -    Maddie obviously not bio-chem major. Mocks labs and flasks
                -    'grounding force'
                -    'intellectual zen' - black circular glasses - delightful
                -    Nikki and PJ (boy) - couple arrive
                -    PJ smartest person I've ever met w/sharp wit
                -    Nikki half Japanese/half white with red dyed hair - beautiful
                -    Nikki - high IQ, high EQ
                -    Dan is missing. Engineering major
                -    Dan "tumbles" into restaurant - low key guy
                -    I notice who they are each as individuals
                -    I notice how they all contribute to cool, nerdy, comfortable group
                     Notice how to minimize input from some, and draw out input from
                     others
                -    finals are done, and all will travel to Seattle for 4 days together at
                     my house before going to their own homes
                -    love that they are happy and relaxed together at my home
                -    they take over the whole place for 4 fun days
                -    love that Libby has this great group of friends
```

Bullet point notes with possible themes circled

Listeners, always remember that you are listening and taking notes in service to the Speaker. If a theme offered doesn't resonate with the Speaker, simply let it go. The best word to describe your mindset during this process is "detached." Your job is to throw out possibilities and proposals. In two seconds, you'll know if they land because you'll see it on the Speaker's face. If the Speaker looks at you like you've got three heads, simply move on to your next proposal. Your first proposal is quickly forgotten and you pose another—in service to your Speaker. Ten seconds later, no one will remember or record the fact that you proposed a discarded idea.

Here's how it might play out: after the Speaker shares the themes she sees, the Scribe might say, "Could one of the themes be navigating all the moving parts?"

If the Speaker pauses and repeats, "Navigating all the moving parts?" like she's trying to figure it out, the Scribe moves on and says something like, "So, maybe it's not that. Maybe it's assessing the current state of play."

In response, the Speaker might say, "Yeah, yeah...assessing the current state of play is more like it. Absolutely." The Speaker won't remember the "navigating all the moving parts" suggestion, and that's fine. The Scribe just moves on and sticks to what resonates with the Speaker. The problem arises when a listener gets wrapped around the axel and tries to prove how the Speaker was "navigating all the moving parts." Drop it, listener; you're in service to the Speaker. No need to refer back to one or more of the stories to demonstrate that your proposed theme is correct or well documented.

PROBE FOR DOING STATEMENTS

The importance of themes isn't the themes themselves; what we really want to learn is what the speakers *does*. Talent is mostly about doing, so to find out what the Speaker does, the listeners need to probe for doing statements. The best technique is to say, "Tell me about [fill in one of the themes]," and then let the Speaker share the actions she takes. When the listeners get the Speaker talking about one of the themes, they should take notes on everything that has to do with "doing" as connected to that theme. For example, the Scribe might say, "Tell me what 'assessing the current state of play' means to you." The Speaker will describe what she means, give a short story, and also speak (like it's fact) that there is a manner in which "assessing the current state of play" takes place. The listeners should catch all of the actions the Speaker describes.

Before the listeners start probing for doing statements, they should watch a ninety-second video on the website to see the technique in action. As they watch the video, the Moderator and Scribe should notice what the Speaker says and what the listeners write down.

For example, the Moderator might say, "Tell me about... always starting out in an underdog position." In response, the Speaker might say, "Well, I noticed I do a ton of research and people mistake that for not knowing what I'm doing."

What doing statement can we glean from the Speaker's response? "I do a ton of research," which we can shorten in the bullet points to "Do a ton of research." The doing statements in the listeners' bullet points should start with an action verb.

Beyond the words themselves, the listeners should catch the energy the Speaker attaches to the doing statements, that is, the energy or excitement the Speaker evidences when sharing what she does. Listeners might somehow highlight these statements in their notes, as these energetic responses will provide insight when they move on to the next stage in chapter 5.

Listeners might also notice that the Speaker starts repeating certain doing statements. For example, the idea of "doing research" may come up in connection with several themes, which is a pretty good clue that no matter what the Speaker does, "doing a lot of research" will most likely be a part of it.

Listeners continue asking the Speaker about themes using this technique, filling in different themes after "Tell me about...," and gathering as many doing statements as they can.

How do you know when you're ready to move on? When you have a list of at least six and as many as fifteen doing statements and you've covered all the themes.

If you run out of themes and you still don't have six doing statements, the listeners can probe for doing statements in other ways. Here are some examples; note that you don't have to use all or even most of these statements. You only need as many as it takes to get the Speaker talking and sharing what she does. For example, the listeners could say,

- Tell me about an enjoyable day at work.
- Tell me what you love to do with your kids.
- Tell me what happens when you feel enthusiastic.
- Tell me how you perform when you're under a tight deadline.
- Tell me about participating in your favorite hobby.
- Tell me about a day at work that felt totally productive and super fun.
- Tell me what you're doing when you're happiest.

Almost any topic will work. Notice some of these prompts use slightly different wording. That's fine. The goal is to capture action; the emotions happy and enthusiastic don't matter.

What if the listeners didn't hear any actions from the Speaker the whole time they were saying "Tell me about... Tell me about..."? Chances are the listeners were doing too much talking, or were somehow editing or censoring the responses in an attempt to steer the Speaker in a specific direction, or weren't hearing the actions embedded in the Speaker's responses, or a combination of these. Remember, listeners: your job is to shut your damn mouth and let the Speaker speak. After you say, "Tell me about...," your job is to listen and write. If your group ends up with a thin list of doing statements, the listeners will have to keep asking and then listen more intently for the Speaker's doing statements.

Once you have a list of doing statements, you are ready for the next step in the process: developing a placeholder for your talent.

Chapter 5

———

DEVELOPING A PLACEHOLDER FOR YOUR TALENT (YOUR WHAT)

"My Genius Talent is creating a safe space where undiscovered talent can flourish and grow, and people who are different can work together productively. I do this by listening, watching, and learning what every person brings to the group; by seeing people's hidden strengths; by acknowledging everyone's value; and then by encouraging them to bring their best ideas in any unpolished form. I do this because I believe diverse groups of people can work together productively and realize the full spectrum of possibilities."

—JULIE L., SEATTLE, WASHINGTON

THE OBJECTIVES

- Learn how to take patterns and themes and develop them into a placeholder or proposal statement.

- Refine the proposal until it is functional and accurate.

You're doing great! You now have what you need to start the first cut on the Speaker's genius talent statement. The goal at this stage is to develop a thematically or direction-ally accurate starter version of the Speaker's talent, not a super accurate, beautiful, or powerful version. Themati-cally accurate serves our purposes well and can be found much quicker than a perfectionist's version. Our process is continually self-correcting and evolving, so getting something functional will move the process forward, and that starter version will improve all the way along.

You can think of your genius talent in one of two ways: it's either the greatest gift of talent you received from God or your higher power, or if you don't believe in that, it's the genetic lottery pick you received at birth. Either way, it's part of your DNA. You got what you got, and you cannot ask for a do-over. As with your hair color or the shape of your ears, your talent will not change because you wish it were different or you like someone else's better.

The first step in moving from a robust discussion of themes and doing clauses to developing a placeholder is to ask the Speaker if he has a sense of what his gift of talent might be. The Moderator should ask the following question and then give the Speaker a chance to respond:

> Okay, thanks for your hard work there. Here's an unfair and long-shot question to start our conversation: Do you have a sense of what your genius talent might be? Only one out of ten people tend to know what it is at this point, so you're not alone if you don't.

Most Speakers will say they don't have a clue, but if the Speaker does have a sense of what his talent is, the Moderator or Scribe can tease it out by asking leading questions, such as "So, walk me through that" or "Tell me what that looks like." After the Speaker responds, the listener says, "Oh, that's interesting. It sounds like you do _____ and _____ and _____."

Whether the Speaker thinks he knows his talent or not, the next step is the same: the listeners help the Speaker begin to form a proposal, or placeholder, for the talent he received.

FORMING A PROPOSAL

It's very important that the listeners continue to employ a detached mindset or operating context in this step, just as they did when they proposed themes and patterns.

Once again, listeners act in service to the Speaker. They should not be wedded to their genius talent proposals or debate individual words or phrases. Besides, if the listeners just recently met this person, how can they really know his talent without exploring? If a Speaker doesn't respond favorably to a proposal, listeners simply let it go and move on. They don't argue or try to prove how that proposed talent really does show up in all three stories or in the accumulation of doing clauses. Instead, they should simply phrase the proposed idea in a different way.

The Moderator says to the Speaker,

> Okay, our job is to make proposals regarding your genius talent. We will suggest a talent that we suspect is thematically correct. Here's how we'd like you to answer: If the proposal sounds accurate or close to accurate, please restate it. If the proposal is on the right track, please restate it so that it includes your language, not our paraphrase. And if the proposal is not even close, just tell us that, too.

Listeners, you will again take notes. This time, however, you want to capture the whole statement, exactly as the Speaker says it. When the Speaker takes one of the listener's proposals and restates it in his own words, that's the version you want to capture—the Speaker's words, not the original proposal.

If the listeners were truly listening to the Speaker's responses to "Tell me about..., Tell me about...," they will have a solid list of doing statements as the basis for forming a proposal. Listeners don't really need to write down any proposals. They simply look at the list of doing statements, reflect on the ones the Speaker seems energetically most attached to, and form the proposal from that. It's usually easier and faster for the brain to verbally iterate a proposal without writing it down first. Also, when we write things down, the brain tends to hold on to those ideas more than verbal, and we want the listeners to simply throw out proposals without getting attached.

Forming proposals from doing statements takes a bit of intuition and creativity, and listeners might find it challenging at first. The great thing is that there are no wrong answers; there's no such thing as a bad proposal. Every proposal moves the process forward, either because it's accepted or because it shows the listeners they need to offer something in a different direction.

Listeners, when you make your proposals, start using the same linguistic frame each time and state it from the Speaker's point of view:

My genius talent is...

When you add the action after that opener, use the -ing

form of the verb; for example, you might say, "My genius talent is *creating*..." instead of "My genius talent is *to create*..." Here's an example of how this conversation might play out, when the Scribe makes a proposal and the Speaker thinks it's on the right track:

> Scribe: My genius talent is clarifying complex problems so that people can take effective action.
>
> Speaker: Yeah, but it's more than that. What I really do is synthesize.
>
> Scribe: Okay, synthesizing, not clarifying. So, what do you synthesize?
>
> Speaker: So, my genius talent is synthesizing complex ideas so that people view them as one fluid concept.

Notice how the Scribe isn't arguing for the original statement; she is simply taking notes, asking questions, helping the Speaker formulate and develop *his* proposal in *his* own words. Once again, the Scribe is acting in service to the Speaker. The Speaker cleans up the statement, edits it, and puts it in his own language. The proposal is much stronger now because it is in the Speaker's own words. He will hear his language, but he won't hear or understand the listener's language as well as he hears his own. He might also accept one part of the proposal as stated but clean up another part. Part of human nature is that we accept our own ideas much more readily than those pushed upon us. Listeners, be sure to capture the Speaker's ideas and language.

The goal at this stage is to get the Speaker to grab one proposal, and listeners will know which one it is by watching the Speaker when each proposal is made; this is one of the key reasons we do the connection on video conference calls, rather than phone. When the listener offers a proposal and the Speaker mulls it over but can't even respond, she should immediately move on; that one didn't hit home. Likewise, if the Speaker has a blank look on his face after hearing a proposal, the listeners should propose another. This is where remaining detached works well, especially when the conversation might seem a bit uncomfortable. When the listener notices the Speaker's lack of response or blank stare, she can simply say, "It doesn't seem like that one is it" and offer the next proposal. Listeners, keep the conversation moving.

When a proposal hits home for the Speaker, listeners will see him perk up a little. When that happens, one of the listeners can ask him to restate the proposal in his own words. That conversation often goes like this:

Moderator: How would you state that one?

Speaker: Oh, it was good just the way you said it. It's really good.

Moderator: Okay, please say it the way you would say it.

When the Speaker says it was good "just the way you said it," he might be agreeing to be polite. But we don't want him to be polite. We don't want him to take the listener's proposal because it's in the listener's language. That's the key: the Speaker must voice the proposal and his talent in his own language. The Speaker's language might be subtly different or quite a bit different—even if the theme does not change at all. Listeners, be sure to capture the Speaker's iteration!

Sometimes the Speaker hears the proposal and really likes it, but when asked to restate it, he can't remember it all. That's okay. The listener can ask if the Speaker wants the proposal repeated. Even if the listener doesn't repeat the proposal in the exact same words, that's fine. The Speaker still hears the ideas a second time. After repeating the proposal, the listener can say, "Okay, say it how you would say it." When the Speaker puts the proposal in his own words, the listeners take notes and capture his language exactly. That is the perfect way to capture a placeholder or proposal for the talent: when the Speaker likes it and restates it.

It might take two or three rounds to land on a proposal,

which will take a few minutes. The faster or more fluid this process goes, the better. At this point, the proposal doesn't have to be eloquent or polished. It could be something as simple as "My genius talent is simplifying complex ideas." The Speaker may worry that a simple statement like this isn't beautiful or powerful like the examples in the appendix, but it doesn't have to be beautiful and powerful yet. It's easier to build on a simple proposal than to modify a complex one that really doesn't work. It's also easier to find a simple theme than to find perfection at the initial proposal stage.

Here's where it can get tricky: Let's say the Moderator offers one proposal, but the Speaker doesn't react. Then the Scribe offers a proposal, but the Speaker doesn't react to that either. The two listeners might feel stuck at this point. The key is to keep moving forward. The proposals offered don't have to be fabulous; they just have to get the Speaker to respond. For example, after both listeners have offered proposals that don't hit home, one of them might throw out something half-baked and completely inaccurate, but it still might cause the Speaker to rebut the idea and move toward an accurate proposal:

Moderator: Okay, those didn't work. How about this: My genius talent is judging people harshly, accurately, and unfairly.

Speaker: Well, I don't do that at all, but I do notice nuances about people that help them learn and grow.

We rarely have a situation like this, but even if a listener offers something way off track, the goal is still the same: capture the Speaker's response. Listeners, proposing language that is 180 degrees in the opposite direction is a good tool if you get stuck and cannot figure out another proposal that is thematically accurate. It also provides levity for your conversation.

Forming a proposal should take around thirty minutes. If your commando squad is forty-minutes in and nowhere close to forming a placeholder, consider hiring a facilitator to finish part I with the first Speaker so you can keep the process moving and lessen the frustration factor.

REFINING THE PROPOSAL

To aid the refining process, here are a few tips for listeners and the Speaker.

TIPS FOR THE LISTENERS

Listeners, there are only two things you can do wrong at this stage: (1) argue with the Speaker over the merits of your own proposal, and (2) allow the conversation to hit a dead stop for too long. You don't get points or a medal if the Speaker adopts your proposal. In the end, no one will remember who made the proposal and no one will care. However, you will all celebrate the fact that the Speaker uncovered his genius talent. As a listener, you are in service to the Speaker throughout the discovery process. Keeping the process moving forward is much more helpful than nailing the perfect proposal as the most valuable player.

Remember, you guys are rookies. Give yourselves a break. You don't have to be perfect. If you get the Speaker to put a proposal in his own words, you've done your job well, even if the path there wasn't perfect.

If the Speaker gets stuck and doesn't know how to make his proposal more specific, you can ask questions. When you do so, it's better to give two options, rather than to ask open-ended questions. Think of a conversation with the optometrist:

Optometrist: Is your vision clearer with lens one or two?

Patient: It's two.

Optometrist: How about now; is it two or three?

Patient: It's still two.

Optometrist: And here, is it two or four?

Here's what offering choices might look like in the process of refining a genius talent proposal:

> Moderator: Okay. You've said, "My genius talent is helping people do this, that, and the other." Do you help ambitious people or forgotten people?

> Speaker: You know, my interest is only working with ambitious people. I hate working with whiners and complainers.

> Moderator: Great. Walk me through how you help ambitious people.

> Speaker: Well, learners are ambitious, and I do this, this, and this.

By simply offering a choice (Do you help ambitious or forgotten people?) instead of an open-ended question (What kind of people do you like to help?), the Moderator has moved the process ahead and helped the Speaker refine and clarify his proposal. Even if the two options offered are wrong, the Speaker will generally provide the correct word choices. He might say he helps movers and shakers or homeless children.

Chances are, the Speaker will begin to realize that by identifying and limiting his audience, his talent is much more powerful and it simply will not work well with the wrong audience. That's super helpful to know as the commando squad begins to specify and refine aspects of the Speaker's talent—in this case, the people he works with best.

PRO TIP

One tip for moving the process along quickly and accurately is to "sprint" through options for a key word. Listeners can pick two extremes (ambitious or forgotten, in the case of types of people) and in fifteen seconds or fewer, offer possibilities on a spectrum.

For example, on one end of the spectrum, listeners can "sprint" through the following options:

ambitious
driven
super focused
goal oriented
powerful

Then listeners can sprint through options at the other end (note: this is not a comment on better or worse people; just a different audience):

forgotten
overlooked
downtrodden
undiscovered
misunderstood

Sprinting through options makes it easier for the Speaker to find the correct option—in this case, the specific type of person they like working with. The sprint helps the process flow smoothly and quickly and adds beauty and power to the talent statement.

TIPS FOR THE SPEAKER

Remember, your talent proposal most likely won't start as a perfectly articulated and polished statement. It will go through a process of refinement as the listeners ask questions and you figure out the most appropriate language for communicating your gift. You're starting with over 90 percent ore, looking for the small percentage of precious metal.

Start simple. At the beginning, your statement might be, "My genius talent is teaching." That's a great start. It's generic, and you'll work with your commando squad to refine it (the upcoming "Functionality Test" section shows how this might work).

In the beginning of the process, many Speakers focus on profession, rather than talent. Keep in mind your talent is something you do in any situation: work, play, volunteering, parenting. Teaching, for example, might be your genius talent if you exercise that gift beyond the classroom as well as in it.

Also remember, the process is continually self-correcting, with multiple stages of enhancement and quality control, so you don't have to get it 100 percent right at this stage. If you use the word *ambitious* now when really you help movers and shakers, that's fine. Eventually you will get to the term *movers and shakers*. You don't have to say movers and shakers right off the bat. We need to be thematically or directionally correct at this point. We don't need eloquence yet. We don't need perfection, because the statement is going to be improved and refined many times before the process ends. One important point is that as the Speaker, you should definitely not be writing—no notes at all! Leave that to the listeners. When ideas are floated verbally, it is much easier for your brain to consider the idea and to move on. Once written (or even worse, typed), those words imprint on your brain in a more fixed way, so moving on from written ideas is much more difficult. You will only write your statement much later on, in the quality control phase described in chapter 7.

THE FUNCTIONALITY TEST

How do you know when the Speaker is ready to move on? The Speaker has a placeholder or proposal that's thematically functional. *Functional* is the key word. The genius talent proposal doesn't have to be eloquent or perfect; it has to be functional at this stage. One quick litmus test for whether it's functional is asking, "Is the proposal wrong?" If the proposal is not inaccurate, if it's reasonable, then you have a functional proposal, and you can move on.

A simple way to enhance the clarity and depth of the functionality test involves asking the Speaker, "What do I (or your audience) get when you perform your talent?"

The conversation might go like this:

Speaker: My genius talent is helping ambitious people learn and grow.

Moderator: Okay, good. Let's say I'm one of those ambitious people. What do I get when you do that?

Speaker: Well, you'll get completely new opportunities in your life.

Moderator: Interesting. I'm getting something different from what you're doing. So, is your genius talent really creating new opportunities for the ambitious people you help?

The Speaker's response shows the Moderator if the talent proposal is functional. In addition, when you factor in what people get from what the Speaker does, it deepens the Speaker's own understanding and changes the language a little bit. Viewing his talent from the perspective of what the audience gets helps the Speaker clarify what he does and what he delivers. This flip in point of view, from what the Speaker does to what the audience receives, usually results in clearer and more powerful language.

Here's an example using the genius talent portion of Julie's statement that opens this chapter:

> My genius talent is creating a safe space where undiscovered talent can flourish and grow, and people who are different can work together productively.

Does this statement pass the beautiful and powerful test? It didn't start this polished and refined. The first proposal sounded more like this:

> My genius talent is encouraging everyone to give their input.

It was simple and thematically correct. When the listeners asked, "What do we receive when you 'encourage everyone to give their input'?" Julie added details, and the statement was improved to include what the audience experiences:

> My genius talent is allowing everyone the opportunity to share their input safely.

From there, the listeners continued asking questions to help Julie refine what she does and what the audience receives. Here's another example of testing functionality, one that also results in moving some words around. If someone starts with a generic placeholder such as "My genius talent is teaching," the question "What do I get when you teach?" can help the Speaker refine his talent into something more specific. If the Speaker says, "Oh, you get this, that, and the other," listeners can propose a new statement of the Speaker's talent using the things people get when the Speaker teaches. For example,

Speaker: My genius talent is teaching.

Moderator: Okay. As your student, what do I get when you're teaching?

Speaker: Oh, you get new ways of looking at a challenge or opportunity.

Moderator: Interesting. What if we replace "teaching" with "creating new ways of looking at challenges and opportunities"? Your genius talent would now sound like this: "My genius talent is creating new ways of looking at challenges and opportunities." Is that more what you do?

Remember: The proposal still doesn't have to be 100 percent correct. It doesn't have to be eloquent. It doesn't even have to be beautiful or powerful. It just can't be directionally or thematically incorrect. It's really a pass/fail test at this point. Is the proposal for the Speaker's genius talent going in the right direction? Is it functional? That's good enough to carry on. Done is better than perfect at this stage, because perfect will take forever. There's no way to know if the proposal is perfect at this point because you don't have all the parts. Those additional parts will continue to create the beauty and power as we move forward.

Once the Speaker has a functional, thematically correct—and not perfect—proposal, it's time to move to the next stage: describing the three-step delivery process.

Chapter 6

THREE-STEP DELIVERY (YOUR HOW)

"My genius talent is seeking out seemingly unattainable goals and creating results that exceed the expectations of myself and others. I do this by intuitively attaching to the highest standard of achievement, by quickly creating excitement while outlining a plan for guaranteed success, and then by relentlessly moving forward until the goal is met. I do this because I know when I am fully committed, I can accomplish anything."

—NICOLE M., CARMEL VALLEY, CALIFORNIA

THE OBJECTIVE

Develop a step-by-step delivery process for how you bring forth your genius talent.

Congratulations! Your Speaker now has a placeholder for her singular gift of talent, and coming up with a placeholder is the toughest part of the process. Things will move more quickly from here. The next step should take you between fifteen and thirty minutes.

Now that the Speaker has her *what*—that is, what gift of genius talent she received—she's now going to identify her *how*: that is, how she brings forth that talent.

Each person's talent itself is serendipitous; none of us have any influence over the gift we were given. However, we have all created and honed our three-step delivery over the course of our life. Five people might have a talent similar to yours, but how you each deliver that talent will be completely unique to you. Through life's challenges, successes, and stumbles, you naturally develop a delivery method, or a functional way that you bring forth your talent. The next step in this discovery process is figuring out your individualized methodology, or your how.

When you articulate your how, you will do so in a framework that starts with a statement of your talent, like this:

My genius talent is...

Then you will follow that statement with three actions, or sequential steps, you take when you are performing your genius talent. You might even have four steps; that's fine. If you find yourself coming up with seven or eight steps, you're probably getting too granular. See if you can combine some of the steps so you end up with three or four. This simplicity and clarity creates more beauty and power than lots of small steps.

These steps will generally follow an order, that is, what you do first, then in the middle, and then at the end. That final step or action is often worded as the effect your talent has on other people—how they learn and grow as a result of what you do. The steps in the talent statements at the beginning of each chapter flow from one to the next and each step connects intuitively to the talent. When you finish this process, your talent statement will have this same continuity and flow.

Those steps, or actions, will be separated by commas, and the last step will be followed by a period. After you come up with the three-step delivery of your talent, your statement will look like this:

My genius talent is [state proposed talent]. I do this by [action step 1], by [action step 2], and then by [action step 3].

Here is the statement from the beginning of the chapter, put into this framework:

> My genius talent is seeking out seemingly unattainable goals and creating results that exceed the expectations of myself and others. I do this by intuitively attaching to the highest standard of achievement, by quickly creating excitement while outlining a plan for guaranteed success, and then by relentlessly moving forward until the goal is met.

After you come up with three to four steps that adequately depict how you deliver your talent, you will have a full proposal of your genius talent. Remember: we're still not looking for a perfect proposal at this point. We just want to have something more functional. We will start the polishing and perfecting process in the next chapter, "Quality Control."

To move from the *what* to the *how* phase, the Moderator repeats the Speaker's current proposal and then starts asking questions. Using one of the sample proposals from chapter 5 as an example, the discussion in your commando squad might look like this:

> Moderator: Okay, this is your current proposal: "My genius talent is helping ambitious people change and grow." Now we're going to put a period at the end of that sentence and

start the second sentence: "I do this by..." and fill in how you do your talent. So, what is the first thing you do when you are helping ambitious people change and grow?

Speaker: Oh, first I ask a ton of questions to figure out the person's end game.

Moderator: Great. So, now we have "My genius talent is helping ambitious people change and grow. I do this by asking a ton of questions to figure out the person's end game." Then what do you do?

Speaker: Next I identify hidden roadblocks that derail progress.

Moderator: Okay. Now we have "My genius talent is helping ambitious people change and grow. I do this by asking a ton of questions to figure out the person's game, by identifying hidden roadblocks that derail progress, and then by..." What's the next thing you do?

The Moderator just keeps asking, and both the Scribe and the Moderator take notes. Generally, the actions the Speaker identifies will be on the list of doing statements gathered in chapter 4. The listeners only refer to the list if the Speaker gets stuck and can't think of additional ways that she delivers her talent.

We normally recommend the Speaker come up with three steps; very rarely, four is fine. If the Speaker comes up with more than four, she should combine them into fewer steps.

Sometimes a person's talent and steps—her what and how—get switched at some point during the discovery process. This will show up subtly and it's easy to test at any point. Let's take the earlier example. Could we swap one of the "how" steps with the proposed genius talent and try that on? Sure. The Speaker will know almost immediately which version is correct. It might sound like this:

> Moderator: Let's swap out one of your steps with your proposed talent. Tell me which is more accurate. "My genius talent is helping ambitious people change and grow. I do this by asking a ton of questions to figure out the person's game, by identifying hidden roadblocks that derail progress, and then by...Or is it "My genius talent is identifying and removing hidden road blocks, such that ambitious people can grow. I do this by..."?

You know you're ready to move on when the Speaker's genius statement contains the talent and three-step delivery in a two-sentence format like this:

My genius talent is partnering with people to help them

change their lives. I do this by listening completely without interruption, by inviting them to relax, and then by helping them feel cared for.

Just as was true in developing the placeholder, this two-part statement still doesn't have to be perfect; we are still very happy with the statement being just functional.

> **PRO TIP**
>
> Every time the Speaker moves on to a new step in the discovery process, the Moderator should read the whole statement from the beginning. This starts the ownership process, which we will discuss more fully in chapter 9.

Chapter 7

———

QUALITY CONTROL

"My genius talent is synthesizing the applicable rules with my own creative judgment to guide a team to their desired outcome they could otherwise not reach. I do this by understanding the team's specific objectives, by assessing the current state of play, by researching alternatives and constraints, and then by navigating all of the missing parts in order to co-create a successful outcome. I do this because I believe that life is like a Class V rapid."

—RIAZ K., PALO ALTO, CALIFORNIA

THE OBJECTIVE

Complete three unique rounds of quality control to refine and polish your genius talent statement.

At this point the Speaker's genius talent proposal probably sounds more functional than eloquent, and that's fine. During this next stage, quality control, we're going to start polishing to bring out more beauty and power. It's a three-step process that involves the Speaker reviewing the full proposal by listening to it, writing it, and then speaking it aloud.

To understand what I mean by beauty and power, think about the waterfalls at Yosemite in May. The temperature is in the mid- to high-seventies, so you can hike near the waterfalls. Because of the snow melt in the park, the waterfalls are raging. They are so powerful that you wouldn't want to get very close, because the force of the raging water could sweep you away and kill you. At the same time, the mist from the waterfalls creates its own beautiful rainbows. Beauty and power, in roughly equal parts, side by side. Nature often contains this combination.

By design, we work on power first. Power in your genius statement really equals an economy of language. If the statement is clunky, long-winded, or too wordy, it loses its power. After we have simple, direct, powerful language, we add a little sex appeal if we need to. First, we skin it down to its most powerful form and then we beautify and enhance.

Listeners, by this point your notes probably look like a battlefield, so take out a clean sheet of paper for the quality control rounds. Changes come fast and furious, even if they are only little edits, and you'll want to be able to see them clearly as you move forward.

ROUND ONE: LISTENING AND REFINING

During the first round of polishing, one of the listeners reads the functional proposal to the Speaker one clause at a time, first focusing on the economy of language and then on beauty. The Speaker simply listens to the words and then reacts and refines. He still does not take notes. Writing involves a different brain function and will come into play during round two of quality control. For now, the Speaker just listens and speaks.

Here's how the conversation might go:

> Moderator: The first clause of your proposal is "My genius talent is leading ambitious people to their highest form of learning and growth, by listening empathetically to what they want to achieve." Does that statement have economy of language? Can anyone read or hear this and understand exactly what it means? Is the message straightforward and direct, a bit like a punch to the gut?

> Speaker: Hmm. "Leading ambitious people to their highest level of meaning and growth." Yeah, that's pretty straight forward. But maybe the statement is a bit too long. What if

we dropped the "by listening empathetically to what they want to achieve" since that might be implied?

Once the Speaker signs off on the economy of language, the Moderator and Scribe might challenge key words to get the Speaker to think—not necessarily to change those words. The listeners offer alternatives as quickly as possible in the sprint activity discussed in chapter 5. The alternatives don't have to be accurate; the goal is simply to challenge the current language to make sure the Speaker has the most precise words.

Here's how that conversation might go:

Moderator: Great, that part passes the power test. Now, does any part need to be enhanced? Is *leading* the right word? If not leading, what could we quickly list as possible alternatives?

Speaker: Huh.

Moderator: If it weren't *leading*, what else could it be. Modeling? Pioneering? Teaching?

Scribe: Showcasing? Setting the example?

Speaker: You know what, *leading* really is the right word.

After the listeners sprint with word options, the Speaker may choose one of the suggested words, or may think of an entirely different word. That's great. The goal is to help the Speaker pick the most precise, powerful, and beautiful word. Then the listeners might challenge another word in the statement and follow the same process. Start with the verbs. Is there a more powerful and specific verb to replace "leading"? Again, do a quick sprint with multiple alternatives. After the verbs, listeners can challenge the "enhancers"—the adjectives and adverbs.

Challenging words and sprinting through options serves to finalize that the Speaker has the best option or to enhance what they have by substituting another word that improves the beauty and power. Two keys to keep in mind: (1) Listening for what feels right is more effective than reading words to figure it out, so the Speaker should still be working verbally and not in writing. (2) Sprints move the process forward much more efficiently and accurately than do long discussions on individual word suggestions. This round of quality control is a gut thing. Scribe and Moderator, you should take notes as you go through each clause, so that you have the newly updated version to read back to the Speaker as you proceed.

After the first clause has been edited for power and beauty, the Moderator reads it followed by the unedited second clause, and then repeats the process of addressing power (economy of language) first and then beauty. Once the first clause gets a full dose of power and beauty, it's easier to match the level of power and beauty in subsequent clauses, and the polishing process usually moves fairly quickly.

In total, round one should take a maximum of fifteen minutes. If your group takes longer, it probably means the Speaker is getting stuck in overthinking, rather than intuitively hearing how the talents fit together. If you're the Speaker, remember to sprint through the word choices from a knowing or feeling place; don't try to over-analyze and get it perfect. Your statement is still a work in progress.

Round one ends with the Moderator reading all four polished clauses together as one statement—the genius talent and the three-step delivery. You now have created what we call your genius talent "proposal": all four clauses, all edited and enhanced, and all cohesive when spoken as one genius talent.

And just like on infomercials, you can almost hear me saying, "But wait! There's more!"

ROUND TWO: WRITING AND ENHANCING

Now, the Speaker can finally take out pen and paper to write down his proposal. No computers! No typing! It's not that we're against technology; it's that word processing and handwriting use different parts of the brain, and we want to tap into the handwriting part. Even if you have horrific handwriting, please write!

The Moderator reads the current polished version like a teacher reading to a fourth-grader: read a little, pause so the Speaker can write, read a little, pause again. In this round, the Moderator reads the whole proposal as it currently stands, all at once, rather than clause by clause. We don't edit for power and beauty this time either. What happens naturally is that the Speaker makes small edits as he writes, hearing words a little bit differently than they were spoken. As he hears the words, his brain says, "That's not how I speak" or "That doesn't make any sense" and intuitively makes the changes, often not even realizing that he is slightly altering words or shortening clauses.

The end result is that the proposal on the page ends up slightly different than what the Moderator speaks and makes better sense to our Speaker.

Round two of quality control goes very quickly, usually less than five minutes.

ROUND THREE: SPEAKING

When the Speaker has written the whole proposal, the Moderator asks him to stand—to take the floor, so to speak—and read the proposal slowly, like a newscaster would. It's crucial that the listeners make notes on any changes in the Speaker's written version; they have not yet heard the subtle changes made one minute ago in the writing stage. I suggest listeners use a different colored pen to cross out words, add new ones, and so on—rather than trying to reword the entire statement. Writing in a different color makes it easier to find the changes the listeners want to ask the Speaker about.

When Speakers stand and read their statement for the first time, they sometimes become emotional. This is the first time they've seen and heard their genius talent statement in writing and the first time they've owned it in a public forum, even if it is just their small commando squad. If the Speaker starts and then pauses to gather himself, the listeners must follow the warning mentioned in chapter 3: don't rescue the Speaker (also known as Shut your damn mouth!). The Speaker is in no danger; he's just emotional. It's crucial that the listeners remain silent and let the Speaker feel what he's feeling. It's the same uncontrollable emotional display shown by an Olympic athlete when, after years of hard work, she stands on the podium and hears her country's anthem played.

After the Speaker reads the proposal aloud, the Moderator asks, *"Is this you?"* This wording is important. The Moderator should not ask, "How does it feel?" or "Does this sound like you?" She should specifically say, *"Is this you?"*

Speakers are generally surprised at how accurate and descriptive the statement is. If for some reason the Speaker can't answer yes to the question, "Is this you?" he will usually point out a small part of the statement that still feels a bit off. The listeners can then ask questions to find out what's not accurate. Usually the Speaker can pick out one point, not the whole proposal, because it's nearly impossible to get through three rounds of quality control and sign off on four different clauses and then come back and say, "It's all a bunch of bullshit."

The Speaker might pick one point and say, "I'm still not comfortable with this word *life-affirming*. It's not me." In that case, the listeners do another round of sprinting through options for the word *life-affirming* until one strikes the Speaker as true, something he would say or that more accurately describes his mindset. That sprint process is quick, usually around thirty seconds.

Round 3 also goes quickly, usually around two minutes.

The goal of the three quality control rounds is for the Speaker to sign off on his proposal as being 60 to 75 percent accurate. When this happens, your commando squad is ready to move on to the *why*. You can also give yourselves a virtual pat on the back. You may not be an Olympic bobsled team, but you have passed an important milestone and you all deserve a virtual medal—tears optional.

Chapter 8

—————

WHAT ABOUT WHY?

"My genius talent is doing whatever is needed to enhance the people and present variables required to create the utmost delight in the result we arrive at together. I do this by collaborating with the project owner to clearly understand the end goal, by owning my authority and observing the strengths and weaknesses of my teammates, and then by inviting inspiration and welcoming changes to polish the path toward the end result. I do this because I truly believe that the music a symphony can make is infinitely more beautiful than the voice of a single violin."

—KARLI M., BOISE, IDAHO

THE OBJECTIVES

- Uncover your core belief or purpose—your why

- Create and attach a why statement to the talent already expressed as a critical third piece

Congratulations, commando squad! Your Speaker now has a polished first cut of her genius talent statement. She knows her singular gift of genius-level talent and how she performs it. But that's not the end. Every person on this planet was given a gift for a reason; in this chapter, the Speaker is going to figure out what that is.

Your why is something you believe in every situation and about every person on every day of your life. It's something you would say no matter who asked and when they asked. It may not be reasonable to others, but it's what you believe, and you live according to that belief.

Your why statement consists of two parts: a simple statement of a core belief, combined with one of your highest values. Figuring out your why should be an intuitive and quick process. This is definitely not a heavy thinking task. You know what you believe, and you're the only person who knows. Often, we simply do not have a platform to announce our why, so it resides in us, unspoken.

Spending too much time at this stage thinking about and

justifying what you think you believe clouds the issue and makes the task of finding your why impossible. Then you end up with what I call a "fortune cookie" why—something processed and inauthentic that doesn't fit you at all and almost always sounds contrived. We simply want to release what you believe, rather than concoct something that belongs to someone else.

If we're trying to decide where to eat, and there are four restaurants closing in fifteen minutes, we have to make a quick decision because if we don't, we miss out. But if it's 7:30 on a Saturday night, we have time to walk around and consider what we're in the mood for.

When we're under a little bit of time stress, we are forced to go to our knowing place. For example, if four restaurants are closing in fifteen minutes, we might choose Chinese because it's close by and we can order quickly because most Chinese restaurants have similar options. Does that mean we like Chinese the best? No, but we know that's the best response in this situation. Giving people lots of time to consider options and speak a belief they intuitively know confuses and confounds the process of finding their why. Better to simply connect with their why and speak it.

CORE BELIEFS

Rather than approach the discovery of why from a think-ing or rational standpoint, the Moderator should lead the Speaker through the following exercise. In his quiet, calm, slow reading-stories-to-my-child-at-bedtime voice, the Moderator says,

> Okay, here's what I'd like you to do. I'd like you to close your eyes again, and then take a couple of deep breaths. We've done a lot of work today. Now we're going to shift gears and slow things down a bit.

> Here's what I'm going to do. I'm going to read your new genius talent statement, and I'm going to finish it with a sentence. This sentence is half done. I want you to finish it with whatever first pops into your head. Ready?

> My genius talent is _____. I do this by_____, by _____, and then by ____. I do this because I believe...

As soon as the Moderator finishes reading this, he shuts his damn mouth. The Speaker probably won't say any-thing right away because she has to articulate what she believes. The listeners will be tempted to offer sugges-tions. Don't! Let the Speaker process the half sentence and offer ideas. Listeners, be ready to capture those thoughts! The Speaker will most likely toss out great ideas, but in a less-than-articulate manner.

The first idea will probably be a little vague and generic, so the listeners should not jump on that. They need to keep quiet and wait. Then the Speaker will offer another reason, more precise than the first one. It's like the Speaker is teasing the reason out of herself. The listeners will know when the Speaker is done. She'll give a version or two and then start vomiting words, trying to elongate the reason and make it better. The listeners will sense the version that holds the most energy for the Speaker.

Usually the central theme of the first two attempts is pretty darn good, and at that point the listeners can jump in and offer cleaner proposals, play with the wording a little, and then quickly, usually within a minute, the Speaker will grab the one that fits.

PRO TIP

Listeners: The Speaker may be a bit worn out at this point and simply agree with what you propose—rather than restate it, hear how it feels, and then sign off on it. Make sure the chosen why is one the Speaker has proposed herself or restated in her own words.

This fundamental belief is in the limbic brain, and those core beliefs—those things you would really die for—don't change much. The problem is that the limbic brain doesn't have language to express that belief. People usually spit out a decent version thematically speaking, and then the listeners can tease it out.

We opened this chapter with Karli's genius talent statement. The *why* in her statement is,

> I do this because I truly believe that the music a symphony can make is infinitely more beautiful than the voice of a single violin.

Karli didn't say it this way on the first try. When the Moderator paused after saying, "I do this because I believe...," Karli said,

> You know, I believe in the strength or the power of an orchestra over an individual player.

The basic theme was there right out of the chute, and then Karli refined it.

That's the first step to uncovering why: the Moderator leaves the sentence hanging and lets the Speaker fill in the reason.

WHEN THE PREFRONTAL NEOCORTEX BLOCKS THE LIMBIC

If the Speaker is struggling to come up with a why and

every option feels contrived or concocted, the commando squad should probably stop for the day. This happens often enough and is not a deterrent or block to progress. What's likely happened is that the Speaker has done too much prefrontal neocortex work in the theme-finding and wordsmithing phases, and she can't quickly jump to the high purpose, intuitive work needed to express her why. After a couple nights' sleep, her why will pop into her head; she'll just know what it is. When you come back together for the next call, invest the first five minutes in cleaning up the first Speaker's why. That will save all of you wasted energy attempting to turn a fortune cookie into an authentic why.

One option to try before stopping for the day is for one of the listeners to make a proposal as they did in earlier sections. If the commando squad goes this route, it is very important for the Speaker to reiterate the suggestion in her own words. Some people are exhausted at this point in the process and just want to get it done, so they accept the listener's language even though it's inauthentic. We don't want the Speaker walking around with a concocted why—concocted by the listeners or by a sense of urgency.

If the Speaker is stuck, one of the listeners could ask, "May I propose a suggestion?" Some speakers may want to go home, sleep on it, and work their way forward. Others may say, "Oh, please, please make a suggestion!" In the latter case, the listener can clean up the language of the Speaker's first attempt or offer a couple of options that thematically fit what the Speaker has already said and then let the Speaker clean it up herself. The chances of the listeners getting the language right are slim to none, but they can certainly stimulate the Speaker's limbic brain.

One pitfall people stumble into when forming their why is that they make it a process with many parts and steps. The why highlights a fundamental belief, not a process. This is one part of the statement where less is more. If you look at the genius statements at the beginning of each chapter and in the appendix, you'll notice the most powerful why statements are short.

When the Speaker owns her why statement, it will be evident in the way she speaks the words as much as in the words themselves. If the Speaker likes the sentiment— and everyone can tell when that happens—you can clean up the words; that's the easy part.

THE LAST STEP IN QUALITY CONTROL

There's one last step to double-check the why, one last bit of quality control. The Moderator reads the genius talent statement back to the Speaker, leaving out the how part (the three-step delivery) in the middle. We're checking to see if the purpose is directly connected to the talent.

In an authentic why, the purpose acts as the fuel for the genius talent. We'll use Karli's statement in the following example of what the Moderator would say:

> Great job on your why. I want to double-check one thing. I want you to check for continuity. We want to make sure the gift of talent and your purpose fit together hand in glove, so I'm going to read your talent without the three-step delivery:
>
> "My genius talent is doing whatever is needed to enhance the people and present variables required to create the utmost delight in the result we arrive at together. I do this because I truly believe that the music a symphony can make is infinitely more beautiful than the voice of a single violin."
>
> Do those fit together well?

Without the how, it's much easier to see that the why is the driver or power behind the gift. It will be obvious to both the Speaker and the listeners. Even if the language is not perfect, it will be clear thematically that one supports the other—or not. If the what and the why don't fit, that will also be clear. In that case, you know the Speaker has a concocted why—something thrown out there to be done. The listeners should simply offer some proposals connected to the Speaker's why themes. If they fit, great.

If not, simply table the completion of this Speaker's why until your next call.

This stage of the talent discovery process ends when the Speaker signs off on this quality control step and agrees that her what and why are in line.

DON'T STOP NOW

Imagine buying a new house. In fact, it's your dream house and you had it built from the ground up, just the way you always wanted it. When it's finished, you walk up to the front door and realize there's a problem: you don't have the key. Without the key, you can't get in and use this incredible home. In a sense, the house is worthless because it can't be used.

Your genius talent is exactly the same. If you've been the Speaker so far, you've just invested a few hours talking, thinking, and polishing to unearth this statement of beauty and power. But if you stop there—if you don't *own* your talent and start using it—then this unique God-given gift is essentially worthless. In a way, knowing your talent and not using it can even be damaging. If you didn't know your genius talent before you started, at least you weren't guilty of ignoring it; you didn't even know what it was. Now that you know exactly what your genius talent consists of, you can actually suffer if you choose not to own its full power.

The next two chapters contain the key to owning your genius talent, articulating it, and putting it to use every day. They can be covered in only ten minutes—a short amount of time to gain some crucial information. Think about it: in just ten minutes, you will have the simple keys to begin owning and using your talent. Why would you possibly stop now?

The only difference is that each person in your commando squad goes through the last two chapters alone, after they have gone through the first eight chapters as the Speaker and have uncovered their genius talent.

This is where your second video call ends. You've all done a great job helping the first Speaker uncover her genius talent. If you have time left on the call, you may choose to start part II from the beginning with the next Speaker, or you may choose to schedule your next call and say goodbye for now.

Whenever you do start the process with the second participant, you'll follow the exact same process, which will most likely go more smoothly and quickly. After all, you are no longer rookies.

PART III

OWN IT VERSUS THINK IT

Well, you did it! You completed the discovery phase and have the first cut of your singular gift of genius talent. You've probably also made new friends for life with your commando squad companions. But unless you read and take action on the next two chapters, you're at great risk for having wasted several hours of your life.

Part III takes your newly uncovered genius talent and helps you begin to put it to great use. Part III is all about ownership and implementation of the talent embedded in your DNA that sets you apart from every other human on the planet. In chapter 9, you'll learn three quick steps for taking ownership of your gift, and in chapter 10, you'll find practical tips for implementing it on a daily basis. When you do that, work becomes more like play and your life takes on new meaning, purpose, and enjoyment. In addition to being a better teammate at work, you'll probably find you are a more useful friend, spouse, and parent because you are living out your genius talent in every interaction.

Are you game to start owning and implementing your new genius talent? Then let's begin.

Chapter 9

———

FULL OWNERSHIP

"My genius talent is showing driven and courageous people the way to achieve their goals and fulfill their dreams. I do this by challenging them to set goals that scare the crap out of them, by getting them really clear on where they are now, and then by finding the best strategies to get them to where they want to be. I do this because, fundamentally, I believe in helping people grow."

—SEAN G., SANTA MONICA, CALIFORNIA

THE OBJECTIVE

Complete three specific actions to start owning and using the power of your genius talent statement.

What if Spiderman wasn't positive his webs were a 100 percent sure thing? What if he worried his web shooters would misfire? Would Spiderman ever go down Broadway, swinging from building to building? No way; he would never leave the first building because if his shooters misfired once, he'd be dead on the pavement, run over by an eighteen-wheeler.

If you're not sure the genius statement you just developed is true and accurate, then you're just like a Spiderman who doesn't believe in his web-shooting ability. You're never going to use your talent if you're not convinced you actually have it and that it actually works 100 percent of the time.

The truth is that your genius talent works *every* time. It's in your DNA. You could wake out of a dead sleep and perform your genius talent without warm-up or prompting. The talent itself isn't limited, but you might put limits on your talent because you don't believe it's true or that you can really use it to do amazing and challenging activities. If you're not convinced your talent will work every time, you won't ever use it. You'll be worried that you might commit to something based on your talent and then realize you're in way over your head. Or you might talk yourself into the idea that you just had a really good commando squad and they helped you pull themes out of your stories. Conversely, you might think you had a really bad commando squad and they didn't know what they were doing when they came up with the proposal for your talent. Excuses can be endless.

The bottom line is this: if you don't believe your talent is as powerful as it is, you will never use it. That's why, even after all of the hard work put in, this is the most important chapter in this book!

You have a decision to make: Do you trust that you do have a talent, that it's beautiful and powerful, and that it needs to come out in the world? Or do you want to put your statement in an envelope, shove it in your desk drawer, and never look at it again? Like many things in life, it's your choice alone which way to play.

MY OWNERSHIP STORY

I learned the first version of my genius talent in 1994; at the time we used the term *best work*. I concocted my statement with a group of seven people, and the accuracy of it was crystal clear to everyone, including me. But for the next five years, I neither consciously nor proactively used my talent. I didn't own it at all.

Then I found myself in a situation where I used my talent—I pulled a miracle out of a seemingly impossible situation— and I recognized that I had done so. To me it seemed like it was the first time I had used my talent in years. I called someone who was in the group that helped me concoct it.

"Hey, I finally used my best damn work!" I told him.

"What do you mean you used your best work? You use it every day," he replied.

"No, I haven't used it in five years."

"What did you do?"

I told him the incident, although now I don't even remember what I did, just that it involved pulling off a seemingly miraculous solution. My friend was pretty impressed, but not at all surprised.

"You do that all the time," he said. "Look, why don't you purposely get yourself into huge trouble, make a promise that's impossible to keep, so you can test the real powers of this thing? And while you're at it, why don't you charge an outrageous sum of money when you pull off the feat?"

I sort of laughed off his challenge and soon forgot about it.

At the time I sold mortgages. One of my clients had a $500,000 tax lien attached to his house for back taxes and had no way of paying what he owed. His monthly payment to the IRS alone was over $10,000, on top of which he had to pay his regular mortgage. You can imagine the financial pressures this created in his marriage and household.

Using my network of family and friends, I loaned the client the money to pay off the IRS in full and eliminated his $10,000-a-month payment. Then I refinanced his home, borrowed the $500,000 out of his equity, and paid off my family and friends. His monthly payment on the new mortgage was almost $9,000 a month lower than the old mortgage and the IRS payment. My client was amazed and told me I had saved his family because he would have gone into foreclosure and probably gotten divorced. The IRS agent handling my client's case was happy, because he got credit for collecting $500,000, and he quietly started referring similar high-dollar collection cases to me—even though the IRS doesn't give referrals. Officially, at least.

I repeated this feat over and over, using the same pool of money for a short-term loan to pay off the IRS and then refinanced the home and replenished our pool of funds to use again. Every one of these clients told me the same thing, "You saved our family. It's a miracle." A solution that was so obvious to me had been seemingly impossible to others, as well as technically not doable, per the official IRS "no referrals" policy.

When I started getting referrals from the IRS and heard clients repeatedly tell me I had performed a miracle, I had an aha moment: for the first time, I truly owned my genius talent as something that other people simply could not pull off, and I started using it consciously. And charging for it as well, since I had no competitors.

THE IMPORTANCE OF OWNERSHIP

With the first 2,000 people who went through the talent discovery process, we made the mistake of assuming people would start using their genius talent once they discovered it. It seemed obvious to us that people would go straight from discovery to implementation. What possible reasons would they have to not begin utilizing their incredible advantage—their super power, if you will? Perhaps like me, they didn't hold their talent as something to be used proactively. Perhaps they believed other people could perform the same talent, that it wasn't really that special and unique.

We all have access to the same information. For example, if five people search "How do I lose twenty pounds?" they will all receive the same information. The information alone doesn't make you lose twenty pounds. Implementing that information—changing your diet and working out—allows you to lose twenty pounds. As Derek Silvers remarked, "If [more] information was the answer, then we'd all be billionaires with perfect abs."

Paul Leboffe, one of my co-founding partners, realized we had missed a key factor: a bridge step between discovery and implementation called "ownership." Simply put, if you don't own the power of your genius talent, you'll never use it. Simple as that!

Paul and I were frustrated that people weren't implementing their talent. Our clients were scared—scared that we had teased something out of them that was an anomaly and not ingrained in every cell of their body. Like me for several years, they assumed that luck or the perfect storm of circumstances conspired to help them achieve a non-duplicatable result.

Because they didn't own their talent, they couldn't own the power and beauty of it. They never moved on to implementation, so the discovery process was essentially a complete waste of time and effort.

Paul said it like this:

> Not knowing you have a genius talent is like not knowing you have a pebble in your shoe: it's there but you're not aware of it, so you just live life as if it doesn't exist. The pebble in your shoe doesn't bother you; it's just normal. Once you become aware of the pebble, however, it becomes a constant source of pain and discomfort, unless you do something about it. Similarly, once we uncover your genius, we've either given you the greatest gift or done a great disservice because now you know it's there; you know there's

beauty and power inside that you could be using. You might think, "I've got a secret power and I'm a chicken or I'm afraid to use it or I'm stupid." If you know your talent and you're not owning it, that's a bad situation.

Your commando squad partners have given you a metaphorical pebble as a great gift. Either it will bother you, or you'll attempt to ignore it. Like I said, it's a choice.

Out of the discovery, ownership, and implementation, ownership comprises the simplest steps and reigns as the most important piece. You won't implement or use the power of something that you don't own.

You must own the power of your genius talent.

THREE SIMPLE OWNERSHIP STEPS

Lucky for you, we keep the ownership process pretty succinct. Two of the three steps take less than one minute each! In order, here is what we recommend you do to begin the process of owning the full beauty and power of your genius statement.

STEP 1: PUBLISH YOUR FIRST CUT

The first ownership step takes one minute. Publish the first cut of your genius statement, that is, the statement you ended up with in the session with your commando squad. Even after all of the quality control steps, your statement may not feel perfect. It's not. It's a perfect first cut. That's okay! Publish what you have right now; you can always keep polishing on your own. Don't wait until you think it's perfect before you publish it. If you do, you may never publish it, and publishing is a key first step to ownership.

When I say "publish it," I don't mean post it on social media, although you can do that. I mean send it in an email to your commando squad partners; your teammates will celebrate your success as much as you will! Next, post your first cut to the website in the section suggested at www.oneinabillion-book.com. We'd love to see what you came up with. Bonus: we'll send you a gift after you publish it.

STEP 2: START A JOURNAL WITH YOUR ITERATIONS

The second ownership step also takes just one minute. Open a file on our laptop, tablet, desktop, or phone. Put the date at the top along with the words "first cut." And then write the first cut of your statement, the same one you just published on the website. If you're still a bit nervous or uncomfortable with the wording of your first cut, don't worry. It's called a first cut for a reason.

Over the next days, months, and years, add new versions

of your statement as you polish and modify it. Each time you make a change, add the date so you can keep track of the progressively more articulate versions over time. You'll have fun looking back and seeing your statement's growth in power and beauty.

I created my first cut in 1994 and have modified it a little bit on five occasions since then, always as a result of accomplishing something that gave me even more clarity on the talent. The main theme has never changed, but subtle nuances and understanding have. With each modification, I add the new version and date to my document. Each version comes about only because I use my genius talent actively, and when I'm challenged greatly, another key aspect shows up.

STEP 3: GET CRITICAL FEEDBACK, NOT A RUBBER STAMP

This is the most powerful and advanced ownership step. At this point, you can finally involve people who know you really well. At the beginning of the discovery process, it's better to work with people who don't know you so that you have unbiased feedback as you uncover your talent. Since your commando squad partners had no clue as to your genius talent, they held no preconceived notions and no bias; they had no "dog in the fight," if you will. Now that you have your first cut, it's time to employ your family, close friends, a spouse, or business partners—those who would have been poor choices at the beginning, due to their preconceived notions.

Choose three people who know you really well and invite each one out for what I call a sacred conversation. These three people should be the folks you'd call at two in the morning if you're in a Fresno jail and you need $2,500 bail. Ask each person to meet you for a forty-five-minute face-to-face or video conversation where you specifically request "critical feedback" on your first cut.

Please note, you are not looking for these people to be cheerleaders, to rubber stamp what you created, or to pat you on the back. Rather, you want them to ask clarifying questions, challenge specific words or phrases, and essentially try to tear apart your statement—as only loving friends might do. Family, friends, and spouses often read these statements and say, "Wow. How did you get this? This is pretty darn good." They also offer helpful feedback such as "You're using this word here, and I've never heard you say that."

In the end, language matters, and your family is super helpful in *refining* that language rather than creating a first cut. When they create, they can be biased, but when they edit a working draft, they make it stronger on the back end. My suggestion is to not share with each of your people what the others offered, so that you get truly different perspectives. You can evolve your statement after each meeting and bring the latest version with you.

After three meetings with this kind of feedback, you will produce a second iteration of your statement that will be stronger than the first. Add this to your journal as the first revision, noting the date.

One of two things will happen at the end of these three meetings: (1) you get great feedback and incorporate some small changes, developing your new, improved second cut, or (2) all three agree independently that your first cut is spot on, in essence validating the fact that you and your commando partners did a great job on the first attempt. Either way, you will own the power and beauty much more fully after meeting with three people who know you well.

After your three meetings, publish this second cut to the website and add it to the document you created in Step 2.

About half the people who go through the discovery process complete Step 3. Those who do end up with a genius statement they love because people close to them have challenged it, offered critical feedback, and teased out the precise language. It's possible that nothing will change because you and your commando squad nailed it the first time around. That feedback only reinforces how well your talent fits you, which in turn strengthens your ownership of its beauty and power. My guess is that you will most likely get a bit of both—helpful edits and acknowledgment that your talent is spot on.

Once you have that feedback—whether in the form of suggestions and tweaks or affirmation—you know it's right on. And that's when you really own it.

If one of your three people wants to discover their own genius talent, send them to the website. They'll be thankful that you shared the process.

DECISION TIME

You're at a critical decision point. Rarely do we have critical decision points in our lives, but this is one of them. Ask yourself, am I going to live through my gift of genius talent or not? It's a binary, either-or decision. Do I want a life based on the singular gift of genius talent, or do I want to go continue doing things exactly as I have been? Am I going to live a life of genius or am I going to live a life of something that falls just a bit short?

The choice is yours. If you choose to use your talent, chapter 10 can get you started on this incredible journey. Even if you're not sure, the chapter's exercises will help you improve your daily impact and enjoyment.

Chapter 10

ACTION SPEAKS LOUDER THAN WORDS

"My genius talent is producing unimaginably great results. I do this by creating a compelling vision, by enrolling others, and by leading them collaboratively towards their genius. I do this because fundamentally I believe I have been called to live my genius by leading others to their genius."

—PEGGY S., SAN JOSE, CALIFORNIA

THE OBJECTIVE

Take simple, practical, and fun steps to start reshaping where and how you play with the talents you currently possess.

Clients who have implemented their talent often write to

us and say, "You can't believe all I'm doing at work now, because I've gotten rid of everything that's not somehow connected. The only bad days are where I get stuck doing something I can't get out of. But I've gotten rid of much of what I used to do, and I'm having so much more fun. I'm also making more money." That makes perfect sense, because anything connected to your genius you're going to do faster and more easily.

When you decide to live through your genius, you don't have to change your whole life. Simply start asking the question, "Does _____ [you fill in the activity: fixing the leaky faucet, painting the garage, driving kids to practice] take advantage of my genius?" If not, hire it out, delegate it, or just stop doing it all together and notice how the world is not changed much. Remember, it's not that you couldn't struggle through it on a Saturday morning, but it steals your energy. This will be especially true at work, where you'll find yourself saying, "I'm no longer doing this, this, or this."

When you free yourself from activities that have nothing to do with your genius and take up way too much energy, you release energy to be reinvested elsewhere. You start replacing the worst spent energy of your day with something creative and purposeful, something that is fun and has money attached to it. As you systematically drop the worst activities, you'll end up with new "energy robbers" at the bottom of your list; release these as well. We coach many people to do this over the course of three to six months, so that eventually, they upgrade their list to include much higher quality activities.

The critical piece is that you have to make a decision and begin to take action. It's your choice. If you've made that choice, take the first step in implementation and play defense.

DEFENSE FIRST: GETTING RID OF THE CRAP

Life is filled with things we all have to do. Driving to and from work, for example, is not your genius talent, but you have to do it. There are other tasks, however, that we trudge through day after day when we really don't have to. We may have convinced ourselves we have to because we haven't figured out who would do it if we didn't, or because we think we cannot afford to hire it out. The question isn't who's going to do this; the question is what would happen if I never did this again in my life? Ask yourself, what action could I take to eliminate this permanently from my to-do list? Most people haven't thought of their tasks that way.

The first implementation step involves asking these questions and getting rid of the crap: things you really don't have to do, tasks that drain your energy, activities that are not at all in line with your genius talent. For me, those drudgery tasks include linear, organization-heavy, monotonous tasks like paying bills. I started unloading anything that wasn't super creative or in my language, as I put it. With paying the bills: I had to sign the checks, because this was before online bill paying, but I didn't have to personally write out the checks or make sure I paid everyone for both businesses, and so on.

I grew up in the Midwest with a straightforward work ethic. We did everything around our own house because it was viewed as our responsibility to do so, and I carried this mindset into my adult life. Hard work was considered a virtue—the sign that you accomplished something, even if it held limited value in the world. For example, I saw it as my responsibility as a homeowner to mow my own lawn, and I used to change the oil on all of our cars. When I started owning my talent, I began asking questions to evaluate why I was doing certain activities and how I could stop. For example, do I really need to mow my own lawn? No. Does my lawn look better because I cut it? No. Can I hire a kid to cut it? Yes. That decision saved me an hour each Saturday, not to mention the mental and physical energy I saved because I stopped thinking about how much I didn't want to mow the lawn. It also improved the quality of my Saturdays, because I could look forward to attending my kids' soccer games or go for a long workout, without having the lawn mowing chore in the back of my mind.

There were many little things like that: I always washed my own windows, cleaned my own gutters, did my own touch-up painting, and handled home repair projects. When I started owning my talent, I thought, *Why the hell am I doing that? I wasn't put on Earth to do that.* Those tasks all have pass/fail requirements, and I'm not a good pass/fail guy. I'm not good at hitting a nail on the stud every time, so when I wanted to hang a picture, I would have four nail holes in the wall because I couldn't get it right. It was frustrating. These were tasks I absolutely should not have been spending time and energy on, so I outsourced them. In my case, I simply mounted an erasable whiteboard in the garage, and anything that had to do with home repairs simply got written on that board— by me or anyone in our household. We lived close to a senior community, and I posted an ad for a handyman. I hired four bored old guys who relished a trip to Home Depot and a day of tinkering. They would come one day each month, fix everything on the list, and simply leave me an invoice from Home Depot and an invoice for their time—at ten dollars an hour! They loved doing these tasks so much, they never charged me for their time at Home Depot! For a very small fee, I bought my Saturdays back, and everything in our home functioned much better, too.

LIST YOUR ENERGETIC ACTIVITIES

Does cutting out the crap work sound appealing? If so,

you might wonder where to start. I suggest making a list of all your activities, then categorizing them by energy level (the level of enjoyment versus drudgery and energizing versus draining) and then by competence level (how well you perform the task). Add a third column for notes to yourself as you consider how to make changes.

Every task in your day—from washing the car to balancing the books at work to driving kids to soccer practice—takes a certain amount of energy and produces a certain level of enjoyment. Some tasks are neutral; in other words, they don't drain you but you don't absolutely love them either. Other activities are firmly at one end of the energy scale or the other: you either dread them with every fiber in your being or you feel energized after participating in them. Do you tend to procrastinate on certain activities? Those are probably the ones that drain your energy most.

You also have a certain skill level in each activity, whether it's a work-related task, a hobby, home repair, or volunteer work. The competence categories I use include incompetent, competent, excellent, and genius level.

Incompetent activities are those you're just not good at; you could practice every day for the rest of your life and still not be great at them. One of my incompetent tasks is paying bills; it would take me half a day to pay all the bills from both companies and my personal bills. I was incompetent at following the protocol for balancing the checkbooks and closing out a month, quarter, or full year functionally, so I ended up paying twice as much in accounting fees at tax time, which caused more frustration and misery in addition to costing me money! You have your own version of these types of activities—you're not good at them and they rob your energy.

Competent activities are those you are able to perform adequately, but not in an exemplary fashion. For example, I like to cook. I spend a half-hour picking out the groceries I'll need for three or four days. I come home, I have the groceries, and I am not worn out or frustrated. When cooking on weeknights for my family, I can perform this task competently and have a neutral amount of energy expenditure. It's fairly relaxing, and my kids like what is served for dinner. However, when my wife and I invite friends over, I can elevate both the appeal and the creativity, and then the energy level rises, too. Creating a memorable menu for special friends gives me energy more than slinging hash on a Tuesday night to hungry kids. For you, it may be the exact opposite: you may be relaxed cooking for your family but completely freaked out and out of your league presenting a high-end meal to guests. It's all dependent upon the intersection of your skill level and the energy given (or robbed) by performing that task.

Excellent activities are tricky. Usually, this list includes activities you have been trained to do at a high level and for which you are often paid. Consider someone who has made a career out of teaching. They're good at their job, they win awards and receive accolades, but they are not energized by the work. In fact, the job, and perhaps the ecosystem of the school politics, has started sapping their energy. If you find yourself frequently talking about when you can retire and do something else, that's a surefire sign that what you might do quite well (excellent capability) has a low energetic appeal; that is, you do not enjoy it much.

Genius talent activities give you energy. You love doing these tasks, and you experience never-ending improvement while performing them. You could do these things all day and every day, because they feel like play, not work. There won't be many items in this list because by definition there are only a few things you do at genius level. Note: these activities show up just as strongly as non-paid activities as they do in your vocation. In fact, some of your favorite activities might appear when you are partnering with a close friend to get them through a tough situation (if that is part of your genius talent) or organizing and running the kids' swim team and all of the parent volunteer assignments. If you thrive at the activity, you enjoy it immensely, and others notice how good you are at it, you are certainly in the vicinity of your genius talent.

PRO TIP

Your genius talent works in every facet of your life. Look at your current activities, whether teaching, practicing law, painting a house, or organizing a garage sale. What's the best way to perform these tasks? It depends on your genius talent. For example, there are hundreds of ways to teach effectively, but for you, there is most likely only one way that gives you energy and accomplishes great results. You can redesign at least parts of your daily activities to include your genius talent.

The energy and competence categories overlap in interesting ways, so that you have excellent skills in some activities you hate and you're horrible at activities that energize you. Those that give you energy but you are not terribly good at, we call hobbies. Bowling, dancing, knitting—all of these might be activities you really enjoy but do not do extremely well. You simply find them relaxing and energizing.

When you create your list, include activities in all the various parts of your life: work, household maintenance (e.g., cooking, cleaning, landscaping, repairs, driving kids to practice), hobbies, volunteer work, parenting, partnering with your spouse, and so on. Anything you spend energy doing should go on this list.

Your list might look something like the following (+ = energizing/enjoyable and – = energy sapping/drudgery; the number of + and – reflects the relative energy/enjoyment or lack thereof):

SKILL LEVEL	ENERGY LEVEL	NOTES
Incompetent		
home repair projects	– – –	Get rid of first!
carpool organization	– – –	Could Liz take over?
email inbox management	– –	Share? Delegate?
Tango	+ + +	Increase lessons
yoga	+ +	At least 3x weekly
Competent		
driving	+	
cooking during the week	+	
golfing	+ + +	Every Saturday?
managing people	– –	
Excellent		
gardening	+ + +	
bookkeeping	– – –	
cooking for fun with friends	+ + +	Monthly dinners!
Genius Talent		
tackling super challenging problems	+ + +	Pick $$$$ challenges
leading people	+ +	Where should I lead?

START CUTTING

Once you finish your list, look for those things that rank in both "I suck at this" (incompetence) and "I hate this activity" (negative energy); in the sample list, those would include home repairs, carpool organization, and email inbox management. Get rid of these activities first because they steal the most energy or frustrate you the most. By definition, these are actually the same thing. If you're frustrated with an activity, it is taking away energy because you're spending at least as much energy on the frustration as well as the activity itself. Get rid of these activities as quickly as possible.

Next, and a bit more challenging, is the process of removing yourself from competent activities you currently perform, perhaps out of necessity. Let's say your responsibility is to grocery shop, meal plan, and cook during the week. You're on a budget, so you exercise caution in what you buy, to avoid overspending. You also have some nutritional requirements and standards. If your skill level in this shopping-planning-cooking task is passing, or just "good enough," then ask yourself, "What if I could remove meal planning and grocery shopping from my to-do list *and* save both money and time? Could I improve my adherence to my own nutritional standards by hiring out the meal planning?"

Asking these questions forces you to consider alternatives that could get you out of meal planning, grocery shopping, cooking—or whatever your "good enough" task might be—all while saving time, spending less money, and/or eliminating the dread factor, which robs you of energy. In so doing, your budget is protected, you recapture hours lost to a job you don't really want to do, and your nutritional standards might even improve: win, win, win.

These competent activities that do not necessarily drain your energy are the most mentally difficult to fire yourself from. If you're stuck, ask this question, "If I no longer had to plan out meals, shop for groceries, and cook dinner every night, what other far more enjoyable activities might I reinvest the time in?" Would you work out in the afternoon instead? Read? Meet up with a friend for coffee weekly? The possibilities are limited only by your preferences.

It's difficult for someone to give up an excellent activity, especially when it is part of a successful career. Let's say your identity, reputation, and income are all tied to a high-level skill or activity that you can perform. I'll take two classically researched examples: divorce attorneys and dentists.

If you think about it, the idea of making your living by having your face in someone else's mouth seems a bit daunting. Likewise, consider fighting with someone's soon-to-be ex-spouse over money, child visitation schedules, and who gets the Lexus.

Both professions require lots of education and lots of skill to become well-paid and well-recognized players. Both also rank as professions with the highest stress rates and highest suicide rates. Why? The professional's daily reality often doesn't match up to expectations, both personally (the job is not at all the fun, fulfilling career expected) and societally (assuming the professional is crushing it financially when he or she is actually drowning in debt). That mismatch creates a completely energy-draining, high-stress daily situation.

Will this person change careers? Unlikely, because she would have to take a major pay cut and walk away from the years of education and experience already invested. This shows up as the classic example of an excellent ability with energy-draining capacity.

As soon as you ditch those energy-sapping activities, you gain all of that wasted energy back and you can reinvest it wherever you want. You'll find there's little you're not getting done because you work efficiently in expending that regained energy. You were spending 50 percent energy to get 10 percent output because it took you forever to mow the lawn or pay the bills. Now you can take that 50 percent of your daily energy and invest it in activities you enjoy, are better at, and get a higher percentage of productivity output for your energy output. Your mood will improve almost immediately, with the realization that you never have to mow the lawn or fold laundry again, and the job might even be done more efficiently than when you did it yourself.

Hobbies are the one incompetent activity you'll probably choose to hold on to. You might be incompetent at yoga, for example, but it's still worth keeping because you find it energizing, relaxing, and enjoyable. Likewise, you might be a terrible golfer, but you enjoy hanging out with your friends, being out in the sunshine, and having a beer afterward. Or maybe you grow tomatoes, even if they are not very good ones. That's okay. You probably aren't trying to produce award-winning tomatoes. You like working in the garden for peace and quiet. You like watching things go from seed to plant to something edible. Even though you're not very good at it, your hobby has a rejuvenating aspect that makes it worth keeping in your schedule. If you were required to be competent or excellent at hobbies, few people would have them. They are simply the place to lose yourself for a while, without the pressure of high performance.

NOW PLAY OFFENSE: TAKE ON TASKS IN YOUR GENIUS TALENT

Great job on freeing up lots of energy, by firing or replacing yourself in activities you are not really needed to perform. Let's celebrate the firing. After all, your talent and performance deserved it!

After you have ditched the drudgery and energy-sapping crap, you're ready for the second implementation step: actively take on tasks that take full advantage of your genius talent. These activities might be paid or unpaid. Either way, they create great value and you love doing them well.

At the advice of my original group that helped me discover my genius talent, I started signing up for stuff for which I got (highly) compensated. Compensation didn't have to be monetary; it included volunteer work where people honored and engaged my genius talent at its full level.

My volunteer work completely changed once I truly owned my talent. I used to run a Little League. Yes, the whole league! Someone asked me to do it because I had run businesses, but I didn't know how to run a Little League, because I could not simply fire or replace incompetent or petty volunteer parents, especially if I had to fill their vacated role. After owning the fuller scope of my talent, I realized not only was running a politically charged organization a complete waste of my time, but I wasn't really adding much value. The Little League needed an organizational whiz with a bit of leadership skill, and much more patience than I held for pettiness. It did not need seemingly impossible outcomes. It needed a saint, or perhaps a martyr!

I also had volunteered with a foundation whose work involved going to a food bank weekly and packing boxes of food for people in need. In that particular endeavor, I worked with well-meaning people like me, who enjoyed a home and three square meals a day, but in the charity work, I never actually interacted with the people who needed and received the food. Anyone could pack boxes. It was a good thing that I helped, but it didn't take advantage of a talent that would have been much better suited for a different part of the charity. Perhaps I could run the year-end gift party, making sure that every person had a personalized gift and every child had a wrapped toy. That might seem like a daunting task for some, but would be a perfect fit for me—certainly more suitable for my talents than packing the boxes in the food distribution warehouse.

Once I took ownership, I came to a crossroads: my life could be about doing work around the house, running a Little League and babysitting political parents, and volunteering for charities I didn't even care about, or my life could be about making a difference using my genius talent. First, I resigned from all of the volunteer leadership posts I had been asked to hold. Then, I took my volunteer work in a completely different direction and started sponsoring orphans in Russia, where three of my adopted children were born.

When orphans turn sixteen in Russia, they "graduate," with no money or family, to a life on the street and an eighth-grade education. To survive, the girls often turn to prostitution and the boys often form small street gangs and steal food from peasant farmers at the open market. I decided to start sponsoring these kids so they could continue their education and buy some time to grow up, get a marketable skill, find a job, and support themselves. People told me it was impossible, especially as a foreigner, but we created a program where kids were housed, fed, and educated for as long as it took them to get certified as a plumber or a hairstylist or in another trade. Using my genius talent to give these kids hope and a future was life affirming for me, and a basic safety net for the students. It was super challenging, really fun, and the perfect fit for me. To date, I still have the only foreign-based, legally chartered, private charity in Russia—an impossible feat due to the politics and paperwork.

If not me, then whom? You might ask yourself this question as well, and consider it only from a talent perspective. Anyone can pack the boxes, and good for them for showing up weekly to do so. Not everyone has the genius talent to forge a partnership between donors, Russian mafia, the federal and local governments, and the orphanages in Russia to help kids in need.

You have your own version of this framework. Play for that big outcome tied to your genius talent, rather than the one that might be offered, which might constitute a poor fit for you.

Professionally, I had been so cluttered down with all the crap that had nothing to do with my genius—household tasks, paying bills for my business, and so on—that I didn't have time to add new markets or pursue new deals. Once I started eliminating the clutter, I had the time and energy to look for "impossible" deals.

Do you have to change jobs or companies to take on tasks in your genius talent? Most likely not. You have to be willing to consider the possibility that you can align your purpose to your company's purpose. Most people don't do this; they just say it won't work. Why not? Why couldn't your purpose be connected to what your company makes or delivers? The question isn't *can* I connect my purpose to my work, but *how?*

If you can't figure out how, ask for help; someone else can probably see more easily how your genius talent can be put to work in your job or your role. If you both conclude that there is no way, however, you might need to look for a different place to work.

In most cases, people with different life purposes or whys can work really well, side by side with no problem; one life purpose will not impede the other, and the two individuals might actually partner well. One person could bring boldness and the other empathy, love, and compassion. In most cases, any reasonable purpose or why connects well with another; you simply have to find out where they do and where there might be gaps with two whys that are divergent in theme.

INVITATION/CHALLENGE

So much of life is a choice. My strong invitation is to choose a life of significance. Choose a life of making a difference. You don't have to change jobs to start living your genius. You don't have to change your title or your salary. Start right where you are. You'll be thrilled that you did.

Are you willing to choose to do that? Most people aren't. Six out of seven people on the planet live in scarcity. From that data, I know that six out of seven people who get their genius will like it—and do almost nothing with it. That's depressing.

What's encouraging is that one in seven do, and their exponential impact tends to influence anywhere from twenty to 200,000 people, depending how high on the power scale they play. They more than make up for the six in seven who choose to stay put.

I think of the horrendously ugly coffee mug one of my kids made in second grade as a Father's Day gift. It didn't rest flat on the table, the handle was crooked and too small for my fingers, and it held only three ounces of coffee, but I used it every single day. When I received that well-intended, customized gift, I could either see it as hideous and ineffective and not use it, or I could honor the gift and use it every single day, thus making the gift more valuable. It's the same with your genius. Once you know what it is, you can either say, "I don't know. I'm a little scared." Or you can honor and appreciate the gift and put it to use.

When you use your gift—when you appreciate it—you make your genius talent more valuable. When you use your genius talent, it holds power, and the more you use it, the more powerful it becomes. At the end of your life, you'll say, "Wow, I got this crazy talent and I was able to do amazing things with it." That constitutes a great life.

CONCLUSION

The book's mission is to connect people with their genius talent and transform their life from simply being responsible to a life filled with great purpose and impact. The goal is to help people uncover their one-in-a-billion talent and put it to use on a daily basis.

I put off writing this book for fifteen years because it seemed impossible. Then my business coach reminded me, "Isn't your genius talent about creating the seemingly impossible?" He was right. If anyone was going to put this discovery process in writing and get people to use it, it was me. I didn't know how it would happen, but once I was reminded that's why I was put on this Earth, writing this impossible book was mine to do. And once I decided to take it on, writing came pretty quickly. That's how talent works—it arrives when you put yourself in the place where it's needed.

The reason I do the seemingly impossible with people, whether through a book or through transformational business coaching, is to create seemingly impossible outcomes in their lives. That feeling of using my talent never gets old! You'll experience the same when you put your genius talent into action.

I didn't write this book just to write another book. I'm not really an author; I much prefer to coach. I wrote it to scale the genius talent discovery process. I want a billion people on the planet to know their genius, because if they do and if they use their talents daily, every problem on the planet will be solved. Problems like homelessness, climate change, and unsafe drinking water are not going to be solved by the UN, some government, an NGO, or a global conference of thinkers. These challenges will be solved by people working in their genius talent and purpose. The solutions will look fairly simple, obvious, and workable to those with the talent to bring them forth, and they will connect to the individuals' specific why. That's how genius talent works.

One of the key concepts behind genius talent is that it equals an activity that you cannot *not* do. If this had not been an impossible book to write, I wouldn't have written it. It was mine to do.

A NOTE FOR THOSE WITH JUSTIFIABLE DOUBTS

Maybe you've read the whole book and you're still a little intimidated about meeting two new people and working through this process that's unlike anything you've ever done. Maybe it looks too hard or time-consuming. Here are a few things to consider:

1. The end result is worth the challenge.
2. The website has plenty of resources: videos, extended pro tips, and more. It is the living, more dynamic version of this book and is updated as we gain more insights and feedback from users.
3. The world awaits the discovery and implementation of your genius talent! Look at the genius statements in the appendix; consider their beauty and power. Doesn't that make you wonder what beautiful and powerful statement you'll have? Yours will be just as unique, just as beautiful, and just as powerful. Readers will envy your talent in the same way that you marvel at some of theirs.

What is the world missing if we miss out on your beauty and power? The world is begging for your beauty and talent to come through. Please go forward. You'll be thrilled you did. Your life will be better, and you'll make a huge impact in the world.

APPENDIX

VICTORIOUS SECRET FASHION SHOW

Every year during the Super Bowl half-time show, Victoria's Secret puts on a fashion show on a different channel. What would attract someone to interrupt hot wings, guacamole, and the Super Bowl half-time show, and change channels to watch the Victoria's Secret show instead? Women are walking around half-naked, which people find interesting. It's also pretty scary for those who are on the runway. Every part of them is on full display.

This appendix is a fashion show of sorts; it's an opportunity for people to strut their stuff in the form of their genius talent statement. This fashion show is victorious, because all of these people found victory—they found their talent and purpose for being on this planet. When you went to the website and published your first cut, you

strutted your stuff as well, so congratulations on participating in our fashion show.

CLIENTS

Like the statements at the beginning of each chapter, the
following come from individuals who hired one of my
trained coaches to take them through a two-hour self-
contained process. If you're interested in discovering
your genius talent in a one-on-one private session with
a coach, go to www.oneinabillionbook.com. You'll be
guided to a code that will give you a nice discount since
you bought the book.

Some of the following statements were created during
an early iteration of the current genius discovery process.
You'll notice these statements are worded a little differently and some are even missing the why statement at
the end.

*My genius talent is understanding how the pieces of a com-
plicated problem fit together and explaining it to others so
they understand it too.*

—ROBERT M., LOS ANGELES, CALIFORNIA

*My genius talent is overcoming uncharted challenges and
turning them into magic. I do this by purposely pausing and
reflecting, by creating and discussing realistic and viable*

options, *by organizing and aligning trusted resources, and then by navigating towards a magical outcome...and celebrating the results.*

—DAVE L., PHOENIX, ARIZONA

My genius talent is leading people to a place that they could not go on their own. I do this by assessing what has to happen, by connecting them clearly with what is possible, and then by persevering thru the inevitable challenges to produce a life changing result. I do this because I feel the world is a better place when everyone is in their unique genius!

—TODD L., NEW YORK, NEW YORK

My genius talent is connecting ambitious people with expansive concepts in a playful manner, in order to entice them to expand and achieve their full potential. I do this by observing and listening for any limiting beliefs or actions, by creating a high state of curiosity, and then by playing a brainstorming game that opens up new possibilities. I do this because I believe you can always choose a different path.

—ALEJANDRA L., MIAMI, FLORIDA

My genius talent is synthesizing the applicable rules with my own creative judgment to guide a team to their desired outcome they could otherwise not reach. I do this by understanding the team's specific objectives, by assessing the current state of play, by researching alternatives and constraints, and then by navigating all of the missing parts in order to co-create a successful outcome. I do this because I believe that life is like a Class V rapid.

—RIAZ K., PALO ALTO, CALIFORNIA

My genius talent is doing whatever is needed to enhance the people and present variables required to create the utmost delight in the result we arrive at together. I do this by collaborating with the project owner to clearly understand the end goal, by owning my authority and observing the strengths and weaknesses of my teammates, and then by inviting inspiration and welcoming changes to polish the path toward the end result. I do this because I truly believe that the music a symphony can make is infinitely more beautiful than the voice of a single violin.

—KARLI M., BOISE, IDAHO

My genius talent is communicating ideas that others simply cannot see. I do this by presenting that idea so it generates enthusiasm and confidence, by coaching them so that the ideas become reality, and then by leaving them to enjoy the results. I do this because life is better lived with enthusiasm.

—HOWARD M., NEW YORK, NEW YORK

My genius talent is seeing what can be, then describing and creating it. I do this by learning the bounds of the field, then rapidly iterating until the new solution arises. Then I tell a story that explains why this matters and how to get started. I do this because I love it.

—TUCKER M., AUSTIN, TEXAS

My genius talent is helping people look past their limiting beliefs to uncover what is possible. I do this by listening without forms, by envisioning the optimal future, and by teaming up to get past the inevitable challenges on the path to success. This is all because I fundamentally believe that we can all have it all.

—GERALD T., NEW YORK, NEW YORK

My genius talent is inspiring others to accomplish greatness. I do this by deciding exactly what it is we want to do, by mapping out a plan that allows us to initialize progress, and by visualizing the final outcome and improvising along the way. I do this because when the lives of those that I can impact work out, I am leading a remarkable life.

—JOSEPH L., NEW YORK, NEW YORK

My genius talent is showing driven and courageous people the way to achieve their goals and fulfill their dreams. I do this by challenging them to set goals that scare the crap out of them, by getting them really clear on where they are now, and then by finding the best strategies to get them to where they want to be. I do this because, fundamentally, I believe in helping people grow.

—SEAN G., SANTA MONICA, CALIFORNIA

My genius talent is creating and accomplishing peak levels of achievement through myself and other high-level performers. I do this by thoroughly analyzing and understanding the task at hand; by methodically organizing, outlining, and prioritizing all the needed steps; and then by relentlessly following, reflecting, and optimizing our execution plan. I do this because I am happiest when I am learning and growing with others towards a challenging goal.

—LOREN H., PHOENIX, ARIZONA

My genius talent is looking at a problem and figuring out the "big win" by deep-diving into the situation, by visualizing a successful outcome, and by intentionally engaging, motivating, and rewarding the necessary people. I do this because that's what I believe we're called to do.

—JULIE S., AUBURN, CALIFORNIA

My genius talent is seeking out seemingly unattainable goals and creating results that exceed the expectations of myself and others. I do this by intuitively attaching to the highest standard of achievement, by quickly creating excitement while outlining a plan for guaranteed success, and then by relentlessly moving forward until the goal is met. I do this because I know when I am fully committed, I can accomplish anything.

—NICOLE M., CARMEL VALLEY, CALIFORNIA

My genius talent is finding winning ideas fast by leading a team in support of a meaningful objective that solves challenging problems. I do this by making a hands-on assessment to define the breakdown as people, processes, or systems; by mapping the initial solutions and creating team buy-in; and then by finding the necessary resources and taking the first step to implementation and then by receiving updates to ensure completion. I do this because I believe in being a good steward of all we have been given by God.

—DAMIEN S., WASHINGTON DC

My genius talent is breaking down barriers to allow people to accomplish their most challenging goals. I do this by connecting with what is most impactful to each person, by brokering alignment to the overall cause, and then by creating dynamic plans to achieve success. I do this because it is amazing what people can accomplish when they believe in what they are doing!

—JONATHAN D., ATLANTA, GEORGIA

My genius talent is connecting with authentic people by humorously sharing just who I am. I do this by asking open-ended questions that reveal commonalities, by understanding the resources around me, and then by suggesting and connecting them with opportunities they might not have considered. I do this because I believe I am at my best when I am sharing my creativity.

—CHIP L., CHICAGO, ILLINOIS

My genius talent is declaring compelling ideas that others bring into existence. I do this by getting really frustrated about a situation, by identifying the problem and address-

ing the limiting belief beneath it, and finally by creating a captivating challenge and surrounding myself with people capable of creating the new reality. I do this because I believe that there is no can't...only won't.

—BILL H., RICHMOND, VIRGINIA

My genius talent is coloring inside and outside of the lines in order to achieve a spectrum of possibility. I do this by exploring the perceived boundaries, by defiantly testing then rapidly pushing those boundaries, and then by acknowledging what has been revealed.

—JIM L., NEW YORK, NEW YORK

My genius talent is inspiring and leading others to realize their own extraordinary life. I do this by immersing myself in optimal environments that facilitate learning and growth, by the continual quest of my own extraordinary life, and by sharing my authentic stories and revelations with the world.

—MICHEL K., SAN DIEGO, CALIFORNIA

My genius talent is providing loving support to others by simplifying, encouraging, and inspiring confidence. I do this because everyone is searching for peace of mind.

—DAVID O., NEW YORK, NEW YORK

My genius statement: The gift that God gave me here on this earth is that I strive to empathize with people as a way to make them better. I do this by: Always showing genuine interest by listening, restating in an effort to communicate understanding, and asking questions to not only gain deeper knowledge but to allow the listener to work through their own solutions, with advice as needed. I am this way because: In my core, I believe that interpersonal relationships can change lives.

—THOMAS M., SALT LAKE CITY, UTAH

My genius talent is connecting people to their soul truth by listening to them with unconditional love, for the purpose of bringing more joy into their lives.

—PAUL L., MIAMI, FLORIDA

My genius talent is combining purpose and personal meaning to create inconceivable realities. I do this by becoming a subject matter expert on the major opportunity or challenge at hand, by creating and considering multiple options, and then by implementing a bulletproof plan that predictably leads to success. I do this because I believe that all problems are solvable.

—EDWARD V., TAMPA, FLORIDA

My genius talent is discovering surprise outcomes by modeling a newly affective mindset. I do this by redesigning the steps of the process used for accomplishing initial results, by taking immediate action to create momentum, and then by adjusting and course-correcting to improve the results. I do this because I believe if you impact those around you, you leave a legacy.

—JOHN R., CHARLOTTE, NORTH CAROLINA

My genius talent is comforting and supporting coachable people to accomplish their highest aspirations. I do this by making the work all about them, by continually developing safety and trust that leads to an ever-strengthening relationship, and then by implementing proven strategies that predictably lead to success!

—DAVID G., LIVINGSTON, NEW JERSEY

My genius talent is moving multiple objectives forward in an unstructured environment. I do this by using the information in front of me to make the best decision possible and executing as required. I do this because I believe there is always more optionality on the table than you can ever see at first glance.

—JAMIE C., SAN FRANCISCO, CALIFORNIA

My genius talent is committing my whole heart into any project to create the most ideal outcome. I do this by helping people adopt a positive change in behaviours, by gently and deliberately encouraging a newly effective mindset, and then by reinforcing those behaviours that result in a big win for everyone. I do this because I always see the best in people.

—LINDSAY W., VANCOUVER, BRITISH COLUMBIA

My genius talent is moving solutions from ideation to realization in order to transport an organization to a game-changing outcome. I do this by formulating a theory based upon disparate data, challenging the prevailing thesis by questioning domain experts, and then by articulating the vision and opportunity for those that choose to participate. I do this because I believe that everyone wants to make an impact and experience the joy of doing something previously perceived as impossible.

—MATT Y., LOS GATOS, CALIFORNIA

My genius talent is helping open-minded people connect with opportunities to create abundance. I do this by telling a humorous story that provides the confidence for them to take action and then relentlessly managing and coordinating the necessary details to create an elegant outcome. I do this because I believe abundance comes from hard work.

—SCOTT W., MINNEAPOLIS, MINNESOTA

My genius talent is connecting hardworking people with what's possible so they can uncover their best version of themselves. I do this by clarifying what it is that they want and identifying what it takes to achieve it by implementing simple habits that begin a forward progress. I also encourage them in what's working and taking the time to celebrate the successes along the way. I do this because I believe people are capable of so much more than they think they are.

—ANGELA L., VISALIA, CALIFORNIA

My genius talent is guiding people to forge their newly desired outcome. I do this by internalizing their raw feelings and emotions, by sensing what challenges they are experiencing, and then by motivating them to start on a journey on a newly found trajectory.

—JOSH B., HIGHLAND PARK, ILLINOIS

BETA READERS

The first group of beta readers followed the process on our initial web-based laboratory, connected with an unhosted commando squad and used the free online tools in their crudest form. You'll find many more examples online.

My genius talent is never giving up on the things I care about, even if they're hard or scary. I do this by embracing adversity, taking methodical steps towards the outcome I want, and trusting myself to stay the course. I do this because it allows me to make the impossible possible.

—DONNIE M., AUSTIN, TEXAS

My genius talent is leading people from confusion to clarity, and from confidence to faith. I do this by establishing strong relationships, challenging people to be their best selves, and then creating a path forward that we do together. I do this because I believe that faith makes anything possible.

—HAL C., SIMI VALLEY, CALIFORNIA

This second group of beta testers initially set out as an unhosted commando squad and eventually hired a professionally trained facilitator for part II of the process—the more challenging part. They realized that high-quality results were worth the investment.

My genius talent is creating a safe space where undiscovered talent can flourish and grow, and people who are different can work together productively. I do this by listening, watching, and learning what every person brings to the group; by seeing people's hidden strengths; by acknowledging everyone's value; and then by encouraging them to bring their best ideas in any unpolished form. I do this because I believe diverse groups of people can work together productively and realize the full spectrum of possibilities.

—JULIE L., SEATTLE, WASHINGTON

My genius talent is creating the resources to change lives. I do this by expecting the extraordinary, by preparing myself for the next open door, and then by taking full advantage of every opportunity. I do this because fundamentally I believe blessings should be shared.

—LAURA P., SAN JOSE, CALIFORNIA

My genius talent is creating relationships that feel like family. I do this by making people feel safe, by knowing what they need, and then by delivering wisdom and care. I do this because, fundamentally, I believe the world is a better place when people serve other people.

—DANNY H., PHOENIX, ARIZONA

My genius talent is producing surprising results. I do this by preparing useful data, by double-checking that things are going in the expected manner, and by connecting the dots with an end in mind. I do this because I fundamentally believe.

—ANITHA R., DALLAS, TEXAS

My genius talent is synthesizing solutions to impossible challenges, visualizing invisible outcomes, so that the receiver may overcome obstacles, solving challenges, and realizing positive outcomes. I do this by gathering data from multiple information sources, assimilating it, and sharing it in simple and powerful ways.

—BRYAN C., SAN JOSE, CALIFORNIA

My genius talent is partnering with people to help them change their lives. I do this by listening completely without interruption, by inviting them to relax, and by helping them feel cared for. I do this because I believe everyone's life can be changed for the better.

—RADHIKA M., MONTEREY, CALIFORNIA

My genius talent is producing unimaginably great results. I do this by creating a compelling vision, by enrolling others, and then by leading them collaboratively towards their genius. I do this because fundamentally I believe I have been called to live my genius by leading others to their genius.

—PEGGY S., SAN JOSE, CALIFORNIA

My genius talent is instigating adventures. I do this by leading with infectious enthusiasm, by paying attention to what inspires other people, by recognizing potential adventures, and then by accepting whatever shows up along the way. I do this because happiness should be shared.

—RACHEL M., PORTLAND, OREGON

My genius talent is granting being, or the ability to create a safe space for me and others to be our genuine selves. I do this by being fully present in the moment, by being truly curious about others, by suspending all judgment, by embracing our differences, and then by valuing our deep personal connections. I do this because I fundamentally believe authenticity creates meaning and purpose in our lives.

—RYAN B., PORTLAND, OREGON

My genius talent is partnering with high achievers to get the one thing they want they can't see yet. I do this by helping them accept where they are right now, uncover their limiting believes and fears, understand what they want next, and then challenge them to make a courageous choice.

—JENN L., ALBERTA, CANADA

The last group of beta readers waded into the swamp with gators, and we haven't heard from them since.

ACKNOWLEDGMENTS

If you have gotten this far, you already know that more than a book, *One in a Billion* is a call to action. Like riding a bike, you cannot find your talent simply by understanding, studying, or embracing the theory. You really do need to get out and probably fall a couple of times before you accomplish your goal. You'll experience the same thrill a child does when he finally rides a bike for the first time.

My first acknowledgment is to you, the reader and your commando squad participants, who invested the time, energy, and mostly the courage to take on the prospect of a more powerful life. My sincere thanks for interacting with the online process, succeeding, perhaps struggling a bit, and then offering feedback that helps the next person in their quest.

Secondly, an entire team of terrific people at Scribe Media

partnered with me and kept me on track to write the book and build out the web portal on schedule, and with minimal disruption to my actual work of coaching clients.

Gail Fay was the scribe in my case, and she and I worked pretty seamlessly, playfully, and efficiently to tease the book out of me. Gail showed the patience required to manage the process with a nonlinear thinker like myself. She even lied to me about deadlines, perhaps suspecting that I was more likely the kid who copied someone else's homework on the school bus, rather than the kid who completed it on time on his own. Regardless, she gently led me forward, never biting off too much at a time, and made progress at a rather alarming pace. Thank you, Gail, for exercising your genius talent!

Tucker Max initially invited me to consider his brilliant platform that essentially supports the idea that stories are better told by people who do things and create results, than by those who complete a ten-year study but have never worked in the real world. Actually, he never quite said that, but that was what I heard: that entrepreneurs should write books, if they can just figure out the time issue. Well, there are at least three more books forthcoming, mostly due to the simplicity of Tucker's platform—that the scribe writes my voice, rather than me sitting and typing. Thank you, Tucker. To the extent that this book changes lives, it lives in large part due to the platform you have created—for myself and for other authors with value to share, but even more for the readers impacted by the wisdom shared.

James Timberlake and Libby Allen partnered as my publishing managers (it usually takes more than one adult to manage me) and helped to resolve small and not-so-small challenges all along the way. James and Libby, thank you for clearing the way, such that I could focus on my role only, rather than how to maneuver in an industry I am unfamiliar with. You made the entire process run without visible hiccups, even though I know you were dealing with them behind the scenes.

Cindy Curtis and Erin Tyler created multiple versions of the front book cover, and I love what they came up with! Rather than choose the best option among duds, I had to pick one of several fabulous cover options. This is all due to their creative insights as to how they could display the concept on the book in one picture.

Zach Obront was my initial contact at Scribe and actually served as the publicist on my first book, *The Motivation Trap* (which was not published by Scribe). Like everyone representing Scribe, Zach is not only easy to work with, but downright fun to work with. Zach, thank you for making things way more successful than they otherwise would have been without your personal input.

There are a cast of thousands at Scribe, and probably more than I could name. To JT, Meghan, Kelly, and the entire tribe, keep doing what you do so well!

A special shout out to Taylor Carson, the graphic design artist who did both book and website cartoons, progress meters—anything not specifically in print. Taylor did a terrific job—her first as an independent graphic designer—and her efforts contribute highly to the readers' enjoyment and understanding of the concepts. Essentially, just what a graphic design is supposed to do.

A very special thanks to Brandon Chatham, who led me through the industry that is web design. *One in a Billion* requires a robust web portal to assist readers in their ultimate goal of uncovering their genius talent. Only one problem with that: I know nothing about how to create a website, nor am I well versed in managing someone who does. Brandon introduced me to his team, walked me through what I needed to do to help them work efficiently, and then set his team loose to create an experience for the users I never could have pulled off. He also saved me the grief and money I would have wasted in doing it poorly. Thanks, Brandon, for your tremendous contribution to the readers.

Thank you to the many clients who willingly shared their personal genius talent statements as examples of beauty and power. The book would not have worked very well without these tremendous examples.

To the men of MOTH, who always remain like super-heroes, anonymous. Your encouragement, insistence, guidance, and counsel helped in immeasurable ways. Mostly, you insisted that I keep going and play at a high level, which was much scarier than having to face you at our next gathering! Thank you for the ongoing role you play to keep me on my game.

Among the many people who have walked along-side me in this development of a fairly challenging endeavor—to uncover and articulate an intimate version of genius talent—a group should be acknowledged specifically: Paul Leboffe is and has been a partner in this process since day one. He is more like a brother than a colleague and listens to my impossible (read: crazy) schemes, visualizes outcomes, and always leaves me in a better place than he found me. Thank you, Paul, for your contributions, yes, but even more, for your friendship and collaboration in making this whole process a reality.

Julie Lang, Bobby Bakshi, Janine DeNysschen, Christina Harbridge, Peggy Kerwin, Dyana King, and Danny Hittler are just some of the co-conspirators and collaborators who moved the progress and process forward way faster than it would have without their contributions. Thanks to all for your contributions.

Finally, my wife, Radhika (a.k.a. "Beans"), has encouraged and supported me through more than two years of writing, editing, publishing, and promoting—none of which she signed up for when we met. She always encourages lovingly and gently moves me forward when I need a little push. Thank you, Beans. Your expression of your genius talent reflects in your words and deeds—the inner beauty that you possess.

ABOUT THE AUTHOR

JOHN HITTLER is a transformational business coach and owner of Evoking Genius coaching firm. John's genius talent is creating seemingly impossible outcomes that address multiple and divergent agendas. He has worked with over 200 companies and has helped more than 8,000 people discover their individual genius talent. He's a member of the Forbes Coaches Council, author of *The Motivation Trap*, and an in-demand corporate speaker. John resides in San Jose, California, and is a happily married father of seven, an extreme athlete, and a dedicated volunteer in the field of domestic violence and homelessness. He can be reached at www.evokinggenius.com.

A.   Babe Ruth

2.   Jane Goodall

III.   Leonardo Davinci

d.   Thomas Edison

E.   Mae West

6.   Aristotle

g.   Johann Bach

VIII.   Helen Keller

9.   Beethoven

J.   Ben Franklin

11.   Albert Einstein

XII.   Mozart